THE FURNITURE DESIGNS OF
Chippendale
Hepplewhite and Sheraton

THE FURNITURE DESIGNS OF
Chippendale
Hepplewhite and Sheraton

ARRANGED BY J. MUNRO BELL

WITH AN INTRODUCTION AND CRITICAL ESTIMATE BY
ARTHUR HAYDEN
AUTHOR OF "CHATS ON OLD FURNITURE," ETC. ETC.

AND AN ESSAY BY
CHARLES MESSER STOW

L'ESPERANCE EN DIEU

ARTS & DECORATION BOOK SOCIETY

GENERAL CONTENTS

THE INFLUENCE OF
THE GREAT GEORGIAN DESIGNERS

THROUGHOUT the uneven career of American furniture design three names have always been in its background — Chippendale, Hepplewhite, Sheraton. Sometimes they have stood out clearly, when design was good; sometimes they have retreated far, almost to oblivion, when design was bad. Whatever of good has been wrought in American furniture, it is safe to say, has depended on the influence of one of these three men.

On the threshold of the year 1939 these names are more important than ever to America, in spite of the growth of that style which for lack of a better name we call modern and in spite of the sporadic efforts of decorators to turn attention to Victorian, Regency, Baroque or any other period of the past which they have in their bag of tricks.

Furniture that is made and sold today follows one of two sorts of design: either it is modern, with no touch of the past in its ornamentation, or it is traditional, and traditional means, in the majority of cases, the styles of Chippendale, Hepplewhite or Sheraton.

In the days of the Colonies the first furniture with any pretensions to luxury followed the designs of Chippendale's *Gentleman and Cabinetmaker's Director*. There were subtle changes, of course, variations in proportion, alterations in form as in the case of the highboy (called tallboy in England though Chippendale does not use this name) changes in the style of carving and in construction methods. All these things help to differentiate American from English cabinetmaking and were inevitable in a nation that was beginning to assert its individuality.

The books of the three great Englishmen were used by American cabinetmakers generally, for the Chippendale style was made in Philadelphia and in New England simultaneously, though the best American Chippendale is usually conceded to have been a product of Philadelphia. New England seems to have grasped the principles of lightness and delicacy inherent in Hepplewhite's designs a little more firmly than the rest of the country. New

York appeared to favor the Sheraton mode a little more than other sections.

The three great designers were all geniuses, and of the three Chippendale is accorded the most acclaim, though he really showed less creative ability than the other two. He was the great adapter of all time and because of his genius he could transmute into consistent unity various heterogeneous elements of design. In general his designs came mostly from the Italian Renaissance with a little French and a little Gothic. Hepplewhite and Sheraton based their styles on classic Greece and Rome, but because those nations produced little furniture suitable to copy or adapt, their creative power had to originate forms which they could embellish with classical decorative motifs.

The influence of Chippendale persisted in this country through the Revolution. When the war was ended and trade with England was resumed, it was found that a new style was the fashion there — that exemplified by the work of George Hepplewhite. A little later Sheraton designs arrived and on these, through the subtle variations which American ingenuity could not help making, the style loosely referred to as American-Federal was based.

Antiquarians have wondered sometimes how a vogue in London should so quickly have been adopted in this country in the early days. American craftsmen may have had confidence in their own technical and artistic proficiency but their customers did not. Hence the tradesmen catered to this skepticism by advertising their products "as good as could be had in London" and silversmiths sometimes went to the extent of using pseudo-hall marks to make their work resemble English pieces. Because of this regard for goods of English manufacture, competing American craftsmen were eager to supply new styles as soon as possible after they appeared in England. Assuming that a vessel took a month to reach America, it might have been as little as two months after Chippendale's "Gentleman and Cabinet-Maker's Director" was put aboard a boat that some of the designs therein were made up and shown by Philadelphia or Salem cabinetmakers.

After the Revolution there seems to have been no feeling against English goods. The Hepplewhite book and the Sheraton book came to America as soon as they were published and at once the new English style became the new style of America.

Hepplewhite and Sheraton designs continued to be used in America through the Regency period (1811-20) which itself was based on late Sheraton drawings. Their most famous exponent in America was Duncan Phyfe, though Thomas Connolly in Philadelphia and Michael Allison in New York along with many others not yet identified also based their work on Sheraton's book. Phyfe continued to make well-designed furniture in the Sheraton manner up to the administration of Andrew Jackson, America's first roughneck president. After 1830 the nation's taste sank into a slough of despond which lasted all through the Victorian era and into the twentieth century.

We have Chippendale, Hepplewhite and Sheraton to thank really for pulling us out of this slough. Like all other industrial art, furniture design sank in the nineteenth century to an astounding depth of bad taste which culminated in the Golden Oak period of the 1890s. It was not till the first quarter of the twentieth century was ended that the Renaissance in American furniture design came. Then it began to dawn on certain manufacturers that if they wanted good design they could not do better than to copy eighteenth century styles and the names of Chippendale, Hepplewhite and Sheraton again began to be heard in the land.

At first furniture makers hesitated to reproduce old pieces exactly. The habits of a long period of floundering in design were hard to break. Designers felt that they had to change ornamental motifs, usually by adding something that spoiled the design. They did not realize that the cabinetmakers of the eighteenth century were masters of their craft, which included the artistic as well as the mechanical phase.

Those old workmen had an instinct for good design. Their feeling for right proportion was exact. When they adapted, as when the men of Philadelphia adapted Chippendale's style to highboys and lowboys, their innate good taste kept them from inconsistencies. When they changed the scale of a piece their instinctive sense of proportion obviated ungainly effects. They did not evolve a new style but they were entirely competent to do so if there had been a demand for something that did not emanate from England. In their way they were geniuses and ultimately the realization of that fact struck the furniture trade about fifteen years ago.

Now manufacturers visit museums and private collections seeking pieces to copy and their copies are exact save that occasionally the scale of a piece has to be altered to conform to the space requirements of modern homes. In matters of form, proportion, ornament and detail they strive to follow their models exactly. They have come to realize that Chippendale, Hepplewhite and Sheraton and the American cabinetmakers who used their designs made furniture that will be good style as long as the liking for traditional modes persists.

Chippendale, Hepplewhite and Sheraton are no longer strange names to the general public. It so happens that at present a keen interest in things of the past is gripping the nation and this interest extends powerfully to furnishings of the home. Cultured people have been educated through the efforts of publications and decorators to discriminate between good and bad design and a little education of this sort makes it more imperative. The books of Chippendale's, Hepplewhite's and Sheraton's designs have not been easily accessible. Reprinting them is a real service to the cause of beauty in the American home.

CHARLES MESSER STOW.

November, 1938.

INTRODUCTION

CHIPPENDALE, HEPPLEWHITE AND SHERATON FURNITURE DESIGNS

HERE are many reasons why the second half of the eighteenth century has especial attractions for the connoisseur of English furniture. It was then for the first time that furniture designers and cabinet-makers began to impress their personality upon their work. There is English spirit enough in much of the early Stuart oak furniture, sturdy and national in its conception and treatment. Italian and French influences had begun to divert the steady growth of an English art but the stream of evolution continued in spite of extraneous foreign luxuries.

In Charles II.'s day the fashion for the moment swerved to Portuguese leather-back chairs in compliment to the Queen Consort, Catherine of Braganza. Later the strong Dutch influence of the court of William of Orange had lasting effects on the decoration of the English home. Much of the furniture of that period is as Dutch in origin as the blue Delft jars at Hampton Court. Queen Anne only reigned fourteen years and the style associated with her is the beginning of homely art and interior decoration of a home-loving race. Early Georgian days saw walnut established in succession to the Tudor and Stuart oak. In the opening years of the eighteenth century the claw-and-ball foot made its appearance. It was an adaptation, through Holland, of the Oriental design of the dragon's claw holding a pearl. To go further back it must not be forgotten that before the Civil War interrupted the steady growth of art under Charles I. that the tapestry factory at Mortlake was producing coverings for cushions and chairs and day-beds, and bed-hangings in imitation of Gobelins. One other point must not be omitted; as early as 1715, the second year of Anne's reign, mahogany was in use as a luxurious wood and at Ham House there is a suite of furniture of this date in mahogany.

The time was ripe for the man, and under various influences—the heavy style of solid design, as for instance the wide splat-back chair and settee; the importation of French taste in sweeping rococo ornament; and the fashion for Chinese design introduced by Sir William Chambers—decorative art was inclined to get out of bounds. Thomas Chippendale, with the fine selective faculty with which genius alone is endowed, took from these apparently incongruous materials *motifs* for his designs and welded them in one harmonious whole. His *Director* published in 1754 marks a new era in English design. From his day individuality became the note in furniture.

Up till then, whether it be the age of oak, or the age of walnut, the terms Tudor, Stuart, Jacobean, William and Mary, Anne, or Georgian, are names applied by modern connoisseurs to various styles. After Chippendale furniture began to be classified according to the particular designers or makers.

This volume is a reissue of his celebrated work : "*The Gentleman and Cabinet-Maker's Director, being a large Collection of the most Elegant and Useful Designs of Household Furniture in the Gothic, Chinese, and Modern taste . . . Calculated to improve and refine the present Taste, and suited to the Fancy and Circumstances of Persons in all Degrees of Life.*" The importance of this book of designs cannot be overrated. It was subscribed for in Yorkshire, in Westmorland, in Devon, in Ireland. Copies of it found their way to America and a school of wood-carvers and cabinet-makers at Newport created new traditions.

These books of design are as valuable as the drawings of the old masters. The Leonardo da Vincis, the Albert Dürers, and the Holbeins treasured from Vienna to Windsor are not more suggestive to the young designer, to the student or to the collector than are these books issued in the middle eighteenth century by the greatest masters of English furniture design.

For fifty years the school of Chippendale held sway, from 1730 to 1780. The Hepplewhite school may be reckoned as from about 1775 to 1795, and the Sheraton school from about 1790 to 1805, and behind all was the great and pronounced influence of the Brothers Adam with their absorption of classicism and severe forms coincident with the French chaste classic styles.

In the contemplation of these series of designs it should be borne in mind that Chippendale and his school are the embodiment of form, and that Sheraton and his school are the embodiment of colour, as applied to furniture. Hepplewhite has a relationship to both. He reached his results by form, and he employed marqueterie and the subtleties of Sheraton in many of his effects.

But since the advent of personalities, Chippendale, Hepplewhite and Sheraton are not the only names. All these eighteenth-century volumes of design are becoming scarce and difficult to procure in any state, and consequently rapidly increasing in price. Undoubtedly the rarest of all the books at this time is "*Ince and Mayhew's Household Furniture,*" *consisting of above* 300 *designs in the most elegant taste, both Useful and Ornamental,* 95 *beautifully engraved plates of Hall Chairs, Lanthorns, Staircase Lights, Sideboards, Claw-Tables, Tea Kettle Stands, Bookcases, Secretaires, Library - Steps, Writing Tables, Music Desks, Canopy Beds, French Bed Chairs, Dressing Tables, Book and China Shelves, &c., with descriptions in English and French, Published by Ince and Mayhew, Cabinet-Makers Broad Street, Golden Square in* 1748," that is to say a few years earlier than Chippendale's *Director.* The value of this is now about £60. There is the book of designs by Inigo Jones, Lord Burlington, and Kent, with 53 engraved plates of designs for Chimney-pieces, Ceilings, Sides of Rooms, Piers, etc., executed at Chiswick, Stow, Houghton, etc., published in 1743, which is worth about £3. There is the "*Genteel Household Furniture in the Present Taste by a Society of Upholsterers, Cabinet-Makers &c.,*" published in 1765, with 100 plates, and a second edition with 350 designs on 120 copper-plates containing designs of chairs by Manwaring, Ince, Mayhew, Johnson, and others, this edition sells for £7, 10s. There is "*Works in Architecture*" (R. & J. Adam), published in 1773-1779, containing plates engraved by Bartolozzi, Pastorini, Vivarez, and others, with interiors and designs of Chimney-pieces, Ceilings, Furniture, Metal-work, etc. Volumes i. and ii. of this bring about £30, and they contain designs for Sion House, Lord Mansfield's House at Ken Wood, Sir Watkin Wynn's House in St James' Square, and others, including the Admiralty Offices, Whitehall.

In fact, subsequent to Chippendale's day there was a plethora of books of design, and these as a literature of the subject are of superlative value to the student, the collector, and the connoisseur, each approaching English furniture from his own standpoint. The folly of those who contend that the twentieth century should produce a school of its own is refuted by these old books of design. The evolution of English furniture is well assured. The twentieth century is producing a school. The great hiatus of the Victorian days when, not only in this country but in general, decorative and applied art had sunk to a low level has been bridged over by such volumes as are here reproduced. The student of design, if he be wise, will avoid the nightmare of modern furniture exhibited at the various expositions, display rooms and shops during recent years and will essay to educate his eye with models of the days when men designed in rich and gay profusion for the downright love of their craft. Individuality was killed by the growth of machine-made mouldings, and machine-made art lacks the repose which is so pronounced a feature of eighteenth-century and of earlier work.

The restless cataclysm of design which heralded the nineteenth century, when every ten years had its particular style, boded ill for the steady growth of national art. We catch the note of defiant, almost

INTRODUCTION

strident, rivalry in Sheraton's allusion to Chippendale's work. "As for the designs themselves they are wholly antiquated and laid aside, though possessed of great merit according to the times in which they were executed." But we who are able to survey the field of furniture dispassionately can give to Chippendale what is his, and to Sheraton what is his also, and can value correctly the Brothers Adam with their great and permanent influence, and assign places in relative importance to Hepplewhite, Manwaring, Ince, Mayhew, and the others.

As to what is and what is not original, to quote Sir Roger de Coverley, "much might be said on both sides," but the difference between genius and mediocrity is the appalling lack of the sense of proportion in the latter. A genius such as Chippendale could take details from the Dutch cabinet-maker, from the rococo style of Louis XV., and from the Chinese fretworker, and combine them with perfect harmony into something at once true and beautiful. But he rejected more than he selected. Perhaps it is not so much the art of selection as the art of rejection which counts. It is the true sanity of genius to reject wisely. The mediocre worker seems gifted in selecting the worst features of his prototypes and amplifying them. Johnson's designs after Chippendale are practically caricatures since they embody Chippendale's worst styles and most assailable points in design.

Hence the value to the student in design of being able readily to pass in review the long line of furniture designers covering an appreciable distance of time and the ability to reject the banalities of the early and middle nineteenth century. Books of design issued by such men as Chippendale, Hepplewhite, Sheraton and others, dated, and bearing the authentic impress of the designer with the pride of the craftsman in his conceptions, mark at once with authenticity sharp divisions between the styles. They crystallise the message which each sent forth to his generation. In comparison, each with each, they enable the subtleties of invention and divergence of treatment to be criticised. In point of time they overlap, but in regard to style there are personal idiosyncrasies which stand out. Cabinet-makers up and down the country followed with more or less personal additions the designs of these great masters. For instance, Ireland evolved a Chippendale school of her own, with carving in low relief and native touches of design easily recognisable. The auction-room to-day finds collectors and experts joining issue as to exactitudes of origin. These books of design come therefore as the key to an admittedly golden period in English furniture design.

ARTHUR HAYDEN.

THE GENTLEMAN AND
CABINET-MAKER'S DIRECTOR

THOMAS CHIPPENDALE

A HUNDRED years had seen great changes in English domestic furniture. The year 1750 found Chippendale in full stride. A century earlier the chair was conventional to a degree; there was the Italianised chair which the noble families brought straight from the Continent or had made in this country by foreign workmen. But the early Stuart furniture, such as at Knole, in the possession of Lord Sackville, came to an abrupt end in Puritan days. Gate-leg tables of oak, and stiff straight-back, leather-seated chairs, termed Cromwellian, offended no man. The Stuart chest of drawers and the wide arm-chair, with its rosettes and conventional carving, are a long way from the *finesse* and the well-balanced proportions of Chippendale's ribbon-backed chairs and his fine sweep and exuberance of carving in his bureaus and sideboards.

Between the severer forms of oak and the middle eighteenth century there comes the walnut school with all its diversification of form. The chair, for instance, underwent several changes. Its early straight-back form began to assume various lighter styles. From the leather back of Puritan simplicity or of Portuguese embossed work, it passed through the stage of intricate cane-work in the late Charles II. period and James II. days, and followed later the Dutch models with fiddle-back splats. Immediately prior to Chippendale heavy solid chairs with claw-and-ball feet and massive splats were in vogue. Walnut was mainly the medium, and in the Queen Anne and early Georgian periods lightness and elegance were exceptional. Solidity and homeliness were the prevailing notes. From the days of William, Holland had loomed large on the horizon of English furniture design. It was as though the great school of French design had never been, till Chippendale assimilated what was most suitable for the new mahogany then coming into fashion.

He followed on with true inspiration the Queen Anne and the early Georgian prototypes. He lightened the lines and added balance to the proportions of unwieldy productions of designers with a lesser sense of nicety. Form, symmetry, balance, harmony, these are his keynotes. He revelled in luxurious carving. The hanging wooden curtains at Harewood House are a tribute to his skill as a woodcarver; painted a dull blue, to this day these simulate textile hangings. His ribband-pattern chair backs are at once a revolution in English design. Their lightness, their grace, their elegance, and their due sense of restraint must strike succeeding ages, as they struck his contemporaries, with continued admiration. In his Chinese fretwork for occasional tables and candle-stands the slender supports and dainty character are surprisingly original. He had acclimatised the salient ideas of the French designers, and had welded them to the stable foundations of the Anglo-Dutch school with such mastery of technique, that for the first time in the history of English furniture design Continental makers turned their eyes to this country in admiration of the styles in vogue here and in search of new inspiration.

In producing his designs in the *Director* he admits that they are capable of being pruned to meet the requirements of cabinet-makers. But the style is there, and in many of the great collections examples exist which evidently have been made according to the proportions of these published designs. In regard to the practical value of his designs the working drawings carry their own demonstration. Detail for detail his followers did not accept. The provincial cabinet-maker had more limitations and less experience in his art, consequently the school of Chippendale stretched its arms far and wide, and the " Chippendale style" even in contemporary days, though derivative, was not an exact copy of the master. To quote Goethe, " There are many echoes but few voices." The fifteen copies of the *Director*, for instance, which, according to the published list of subscribers, went to Yorkshire, became the centres of new impulses ; and bearing in mind that eighteenth-century cabinet-makers had a strong personality of their own, these fifteen copies produced something more than mere slavish copyists.

When Chippendale published his *Director* he promulgated ideas in English design the like of which had not penetrated less fashionable centres than London. People of taste took their fashions from town, as is seen from Addison and contemporary literature. The simple family of the Vicar of Wakefield were easily imposed upon by two ladies from town with manners and diction far from elegant. Chippendale was a pioneer, his designs had a wide circulation, and his genius, like that of Josiah Wedgwood, impressed itself on the art of his generation. The originality of Chippendale was merged into the common style of the period, and the publication of his book of designs had not a little to do with eclipsing his own original creations. His followers and imitators were legion. Having once grasped the cardinal points, eighteenth-century cabinet-makers are eager to follow the new mode,—

> Most can raise the flowers now,
> For all have got the seed.

The three styles of Chippendale are clearly defined in the *Director*. The commode-tables (pp. 37-39), the ribband-back chairs and firescreens, the pier-glass frames, and the cornice girandole (p. 14), are as French in origin as the decorations of the *salons* at Versailles under the Regency and later under *Louis Quinze*. What Caffieri executed in graceful curves and chased metal mountings, where fantastic details ran riot in rococo ornament, Chippendale carved in mahogany. His elaborate foliage and the delicacy of his ribbands and love-knots come as a new note in English furniture. What Grinling Gibbons did with ease, with his fruits and his garlands in the soft lime wood, in cornices and mouldings and architectural details, Chippendale recreated in miniature in furniture.

French as is the tenor of his style, everywhere the Chinese incident peeps forth. Some of his designs are admittedly Chinese, as in the fretwork chairs (p. 6), or in the frets and writing-table (pp. 31, 32), or in the hanging china shelves (pp. 33-35). In others it is discernible in small details such as the cornice girandole (p. 14), French in every detail except the apex, which discovers a seated Chinaman in a pagoda. Some of the hanging shelves are almost replicas in form of pendant lamps in Chinese temples. Even the chairs entitled French (p. 9) show in the designs on the tapestry seats the Chinese junk, the drooping willow, and the mandarin figures which were at the time being reproduced on the blue and white Worcester porcelain—and Chippendale was a Worcester man. A set of china cases (p. 49) are as Chinese in conception as though they had been designed by an oriental hand. They are practically pagodas in miniature.

The Gothic style exhibits, as far as the designs go, Chippendale in his least pleasing manner. Horace Walpole, with his stucco, sham, Gothic villa at Strawberry Hill, had a lot to answer for. But among well-known examples of Gothic Chippendale, there are some fine specimens which seem to indicate what Chippendale might have done had he elected to revive the magnificence of the carving, with its delicate tracery which has never been surpassed, of the early English chests of sixteenth-century days.

As to his versatility, the chest of drawers and clothes press (p. 48) stand for absolute simplicity. They are examples of the useful, and are without a vestige of ornament, save a slight suggestion of fretwork in one. Similarly some of his library tables might find a place in a well-furnished office to-day without attracting undue attention in regard to their ornate character.

That in his latter years he could so adapt his flowing style as to work in conjunction with Robert Adam is a tribute to the greatness of Chippendale. The library table at Nostell Priory, Yorkshire, serves as a famous example of his severer classic work under newer inspirations. The chairs designed by Adam for Osterley are another case in point where Chippendale worked on chaster lines.

That he used satinwood and employed the most beautiful inlays of coloured woods and ivory is a proven fact. Twenty years before Sheraton came to London, Chippendale had worked in this manner; and at Harewood House a fine suite of handsome furniture exists, enriched with marqueterie on a glowing satinwood ground, which he executed in co-operation with Robert Adam. The original invoices rendered by "Chippendale, Haig & Co.," in 1773, are still in the possession of Lord Harewood.

Little is known of Thomas Chippendale the first, of Worcester, who migrated to London with his son, the great Thomas Chippendale. But there is a third Thomas Chippendale, who carried on the traditions. The firm was Chippendale, Haig & Co., till about 1796, when the last Thomas Chippendale carried on the business alone at St Martin's Lane, at the Haymarket, and at Jermyn Street. This Thomas Chippendale exhibited five pictures at the Royal Academy, and was known as a fine draughtsman and designer. He died in 1822.

In regard to the work of the great Chippendale and his son, the third Thomas Chippendale, especially of course the father, and their visits to the seats of noblemen, where they took a staff of workmen and personally superintended the work, they introduced into England something of the French thoroughness in combining interior decoration with the prevailing style of furniture. But it was form and symmetry which was the governing note with them and their school. The rise and development of the colourists was to come later. To this day many invoices and accounts for furniture of the eighteenth century are preserved by the descendants of their patrons. Lord St Oswald has a library table made for his ancestors by Chippendale, and the bill for it is religiously kept in one of the drawers :

"To a large mahogany library table, of very fine wood, with doors on each side of the bottom part and drawers within on one side and partitions on the other, with terms to ditto carved and ornamented with lions' heads and paws, with carved ovals in pannels of the doors, and the top covered with black leather, and the whole compleatly finished in the most elegant taste, £72, 10s."

The present value of this table would be, if it were offered at Christie's, something like £2,000. At the recent sale at Holm Lacy, the seat of the Earl of Chesterfield, a Chippendale bookcase realised eighteen hundred guineas.

The Chinese taste of the middle eighteenth century finds its monument in the pagoda of Sir William Chambers at Kew Gardens, and in the willow-pattern plate first produced at Caughley. But Chippendale and the school he founded is still a living influence; there is no more popular term in latter-day furniture styles than "Chippendale." He has been plagiarised, he has been copied, he has been forged. A thousand atrocities

THOMAS CHIPPENDALE

have been perpetrated in his name, " defamed by every charlatan and soiled with all ignoble use," but his memory lives green in the hearts of all lovers of the finest traditions in English furniture. He was the pioneer of the taste of his day, and the lawgiver to the cabinet-makers scattered up and down the country, who rapidly produced good work on his lines ; and his restless virility as a carver, as a designer, and as a master craftsman have won him a niche in the temple of fame.

ARTHUR HAYDEN.

THE
GENTLEMAN
AND
CABINET-MAKER's
DIRECTOR.

BEING A LARGE
COLLECTION
OF THE MOST
Elegant and Useful Designs of Houshold Furniture
IN THE
GOTHIC, CHINESE and MODERN TASTE:

Including a great Variety of

BOOK-CASES for Libraries or Private Rooms,	TEA-CHESTS, TRAYS, FIRE-SCREENS,
COMMODES,	CHAIRS, SETTEES, SOPHA'S, BEDS,
LIBRARY and WRITING-TABLES,	PRESSES and CLOATHS-CHESTS,
BUROES, BREAKFAST-TABLES	PIER-GLASS SCONCES, SLAB FRAMES,
DRESSING and CHINA-TABLES,	BRACKETS, CANDLE-STANDS,
CHINA-CASES, HANGING-SHELVES,	CLOCK-CASES, FRETS,

AND OTHER
ORNAMENTS.
THE WHOLE COMPREHENDED IN
ONE HUNDRED and SIXTY COPPER-PLATES neatly Engraved,

Calculated to improve and refine the present Taste, and suited to
the Fancy and Circumstances of Persons in all Degrees of Life.

Dulcique animos novitate tenebo.—OVID.
Ludentis speciem dabit et torquebitur.—HOR.

BY
THOMAS CHIPPENDALE
Of ST. MARTIN'S LANE, CABINET-MAKER

LONDON,
Printed for the AUTHOR and Sold at his house in St. Martin's Lane.   M.DCCLIV.

Also by T. OSBORNE, Bookseller in Gray's-Inn; H. PIERS, Bookseller, in Holborn; R. SAYER, Printseller in Fleet Street;
J. SWAN, near Northumberland-House, in the Strand; At EDINBURGH by Messrs. HAMILTON and BALFOUR:
and at DUBLIN by Mr. JOHN SMITH, on the Blind-Quay.

THE
PREFACE

OF all the Arts which are either improved or ornamented by Architecture, that of CABINET-MAKING is not only the most useful and ornamental, but capable of receiving as great assistance from it as any whatever. I have therefore prefixed to the following designs a short explanation of the five orders. Without an acquaintance with this science, and some knowledge of the rules of Perspective, the Cabinet-Maker cannot make the designs of his work intelligible, nor shew, in a little compass, the whole conduct and effect of the piece. These, therefore, ought to be carefully studied by every one who would excel in this branch, since they are the very soul and basis of his art.

The Title-Page has already called the following work, *The Gentleman and Cabinet-Maker's Director*, as being calculated to assist the one in the choice, and the other in the execution of the designs; which are so contrived, that if no one drawing should singly answer the Gentleman's taste, there will yet be found a variety of hints sufficient to construct a new one.

I have been encouraged to begin and carry on this work not only (as the puff in the play-bill says) by persons of distinction, but of eminent taste for performances of this sort; who have, upon many occasions, signified some surprize and regret, that an art capable of so much perfection and refinement, should be executed with so little propriety and elegance. How far the following sheets may remove a complaint which I am afraid is not altogether groundless, the judicious reader will determine: I hope, however, the novelty, as well as the usefulness of the performance, will make some atonement for its faults and imperfections. I am sensible there are too many to be found in it; for I frankly confess, that in executing many of the drawings, my pencil has but faintly copied out those images that my fancy suggested, and had they not been published till I could have pronounced them perfect, perhaps they never had seen the light. Nevertheless, I was not upon that account afraid to let them go abroad for I have been told that the greatest masters of every other art have laboured under the same difficulty.

PREFACE

A late writer, of distinguished taste and abilities, speaking of the delicacy of every author of genius with respect to his own performances, observes, that he has the continual mortification to find himself incapable of taking entire possession of that ideal beauty that warms and fills his imagination.

Never, says he (in a quotation from Tully), was any thing more beautiful than the Venus of Apelles, or the Jove of Phidias, yet were they by no means equal to those high notions of beauty which animated the geniuses of those wonderful artists. The case is the same in all arts where taste and imagination are concerned; and I am persuaded that he who can survey his own works with every satisfaction and complacency, will hardly ever find the world of the same favourable opinion with himself.

I am not afraid of the fate an author usually meets with on his first appearance, from a set of critics who are never wanting to shew their wit and malice on the performances of others: I shall repay their censures with contempt. Let them unmolested deal out their pointless abuse, and convince the world they have neither good nature to commend, judgment to correct, nor skill to execute what they find fault with.

The correction of the judicious and impartial I shall always receive with diffidence in my own abilities and respect to theirs. But though the following designs were more perfect than my fondness for my own offspring could ever suppose them, I should yet be far from expecting the united approbation of ALL those whose sentiments have an undoubted claim to be regarded; for a thousand accidental circumstances may concur in dividing the opinions of the most improved judges, and the most unprejudiced will find it difficult to disengage himself from a partial affection to some particular beauties, of which the general course of his studies, or the peculiar cast of his temper may have rendered him most sensible. The mind, when pronouncing judgment upon any work of taste and genius, is apt to decide of its merit according as those circumstances which she most admires either prevail or are deficient. Thus, for instance (says the ingenious author before quoted), the excellency of the *Roman* masters in painting consists in beauty of *design*, nobleness of attitude, and delicacy of expression, but the charms of good *colouring* are wanting: On the contrary, the *Venetian* school is said to have neglected *design* a little too much, but at the same time has been more attentive to the grace and harmony of well-disposed *lights* and *shades*. Now it will be admitted by all admirers of this noble art, that no composition of the pencil can be perfect when either of these qualities are absent; yet the most accomplished judge may be so particularly struck with one or other of these

PREFACE

excellences, in preference to the rest, as to be influenced in his censure or applause of the whole tablature, by the predominacy or deficiency of his favourite beauty. Something of this kind, tho' the following sheets had all the perfection of human composition, would no doubt subject them in many things to the censure of the most approved judges, whose applause I should esteem my greatest honour, and whose correction I shall ever be proud to improve by.

Upon the whole, I have given no design but what may be executed with advantage by the hands of a skilful workman, tho' some of the profession have been diligent enough to represent them (especially those after the Gothic and Chinese manner) as so many specious drawings, impossible to be worked off by any mechanic whatsoever. I will not scruple to attribute this to malice, ignorance, and inability: And I am confident I can convince all Noblemen, Gentlemen, or others, who will honour me with their commands, that every design in the book can be improved, both as to beauty and enrichment, in the execution of it, by

Their Most Obedient Servant,

THOMAS CHIPPENDALE.

ST MARTIN'S LANE,
March 23, 1754.

CONTENTS

CHIPPENDALE

THE GENTLEMAN AND CABINET-MAKER'S DIRECTOR

CONTENTS

CHIPPENDALE

Ribband-back Chairs and Fire Screens

CHIPPENDALE

Chairs, showing various styles for Legs, and Candle Stands

CHIPPENDALE

Chairs, showing various styles for Legs, and Horse Fire Screen

CHIPPENDALE

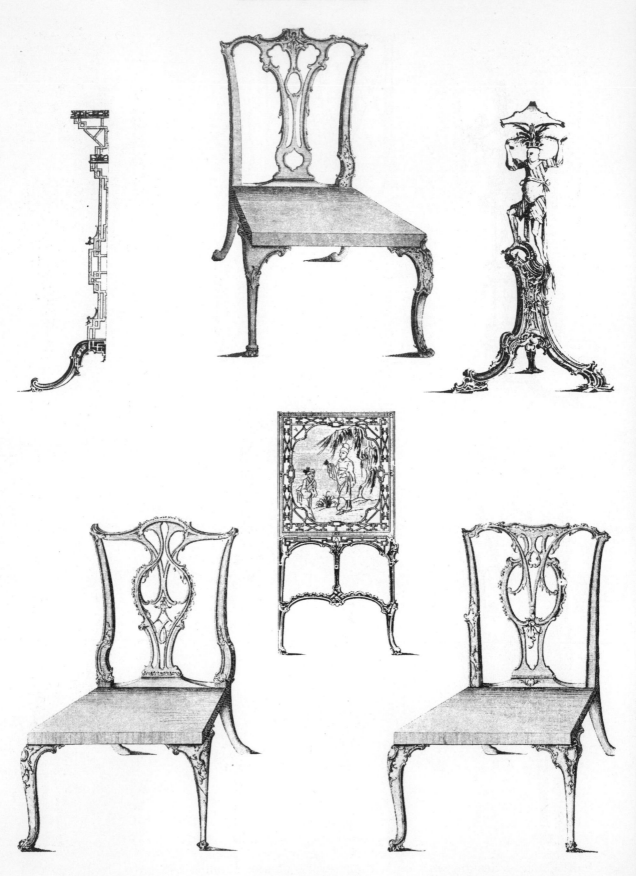

Chairs, showing various styles for Legs, Fire Screens and Candle Stands

CHIPPENDALE

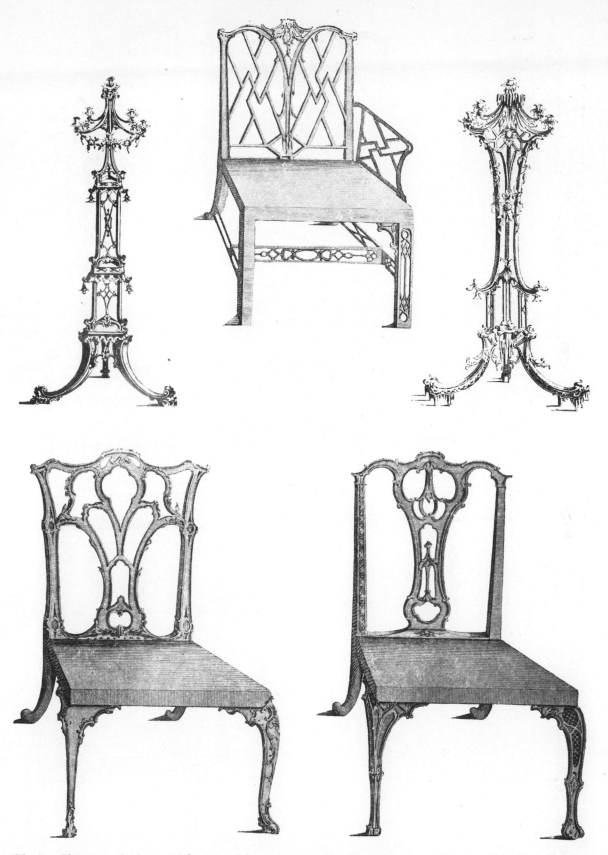

Chair, Chinese design, with or without arms, Candle Stands, and two Chairs showing
a variety of styles for Legs

CHIPPENDALE

Chairs, Chinese design, showing various styles for Legs

CHIPPENDALE

Chairs, Chinese design, and two Gothic, showing various styles for Legs

CHIPPENDALE

Chairs, Gothic design, showing various styles for Legs, and Fire Screen

CHIPPENDALE

French Chairs, with or without arms, and a variety of styles for Legs, and
Horse Fire Screen

CHIPPENDALE

French Chairs, with or without arms, and various styles for Legs, and Girandole

CHIPPENDALE

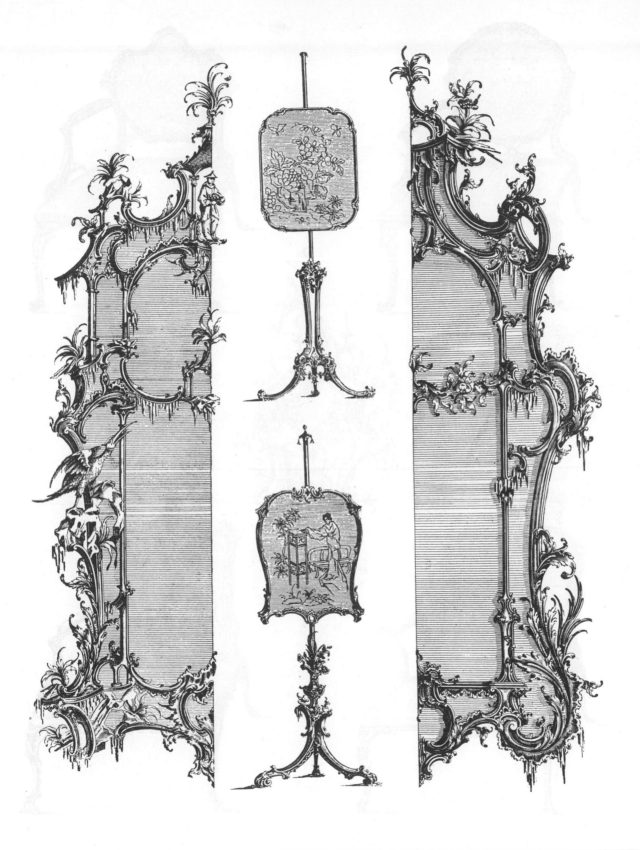

Pier Glass Frames and Fire Screens

CHIPPENDALE

Four designs for Pier Glass Frames, and two Horse Fire Screens

CHIPPENDALE

Girandoles and Pier Glass Frames

CHIPPENDALE

Cornice Girandole, two designs for Pier Glass Frames, and two designs for
Shields for Pediments

CHIPPENDALE

Hanging Shelves, two designs for Pier Glasses, two designs for Shields for
Pediments, and four Brackets for Marble Slabs

CHIPPENDALE

Cornices for Beds or Windows, Shields for Pediments, China Trays and
Table Clock Case

CHIPPENDALE

Girandoles, and Desk and Bookcase

CHIPPENDALE

Desk and Bookcase

CHIPPENDALE

Brackets for Busts, Dressing Chest and Bookcase, Clock Cases, and Bureau Table

CHIPPENDALE

Clock Cases, Desk and Bookcase, Tea Chests, and Bureau Table

CHIPPENDALE

Cornice, Candle Stands, and Desk and Bookcase

CHIPPENDALE

Table Clock Cases, Dressing Chest and Bookcase, China and Breakfast Tables

CHIPPENDALE

Brackets for Marble Slabs, Desk and Bookcase, China and Breakfast Tables

CHIPPENDALE

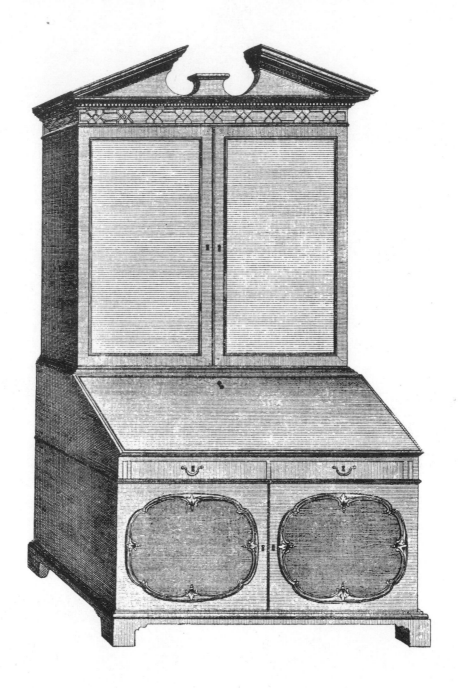

Desk and Bookcase

CHIPPENDALE

China Case and Sideboard Table

CHIPPENDALE

China Case, Sideboard Table, and Clothes Press

CHIPPENDALE

Brackets for Busts, Cabinet, Tea Chest, and Sideboard Table

CHIPPENDALE

Commode Clothes Press, Sideboard Table, and Tea Chest

CHIPPENDALE

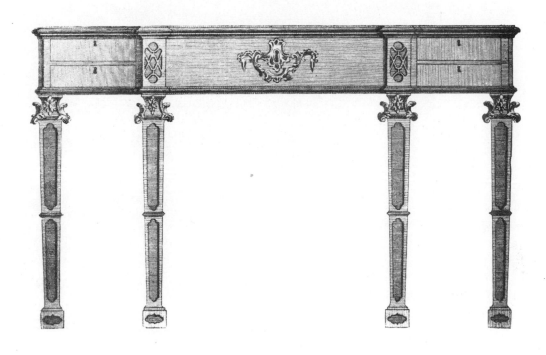

Writing and Sideboard Tables

CHIPPENDALE

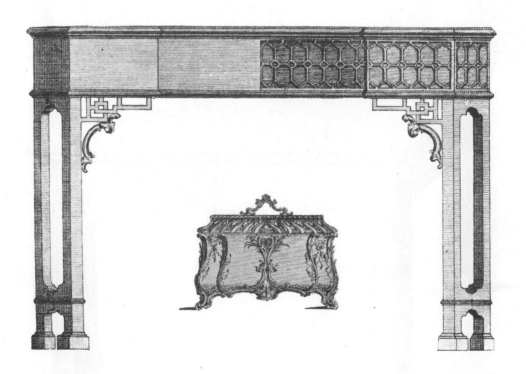

Sideboard and Writing Tables, and Tea Chest

CHIPPENDALE

Frets, and Writing Table

CHIPPENDALE

Frets

CHIPPENDALE

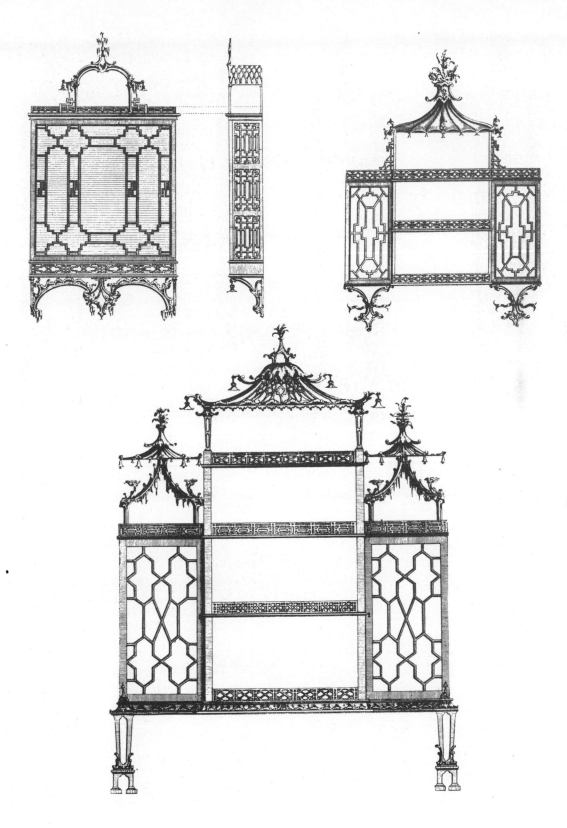

Hanging Shelves and China Shelf

CHIPPENDALE

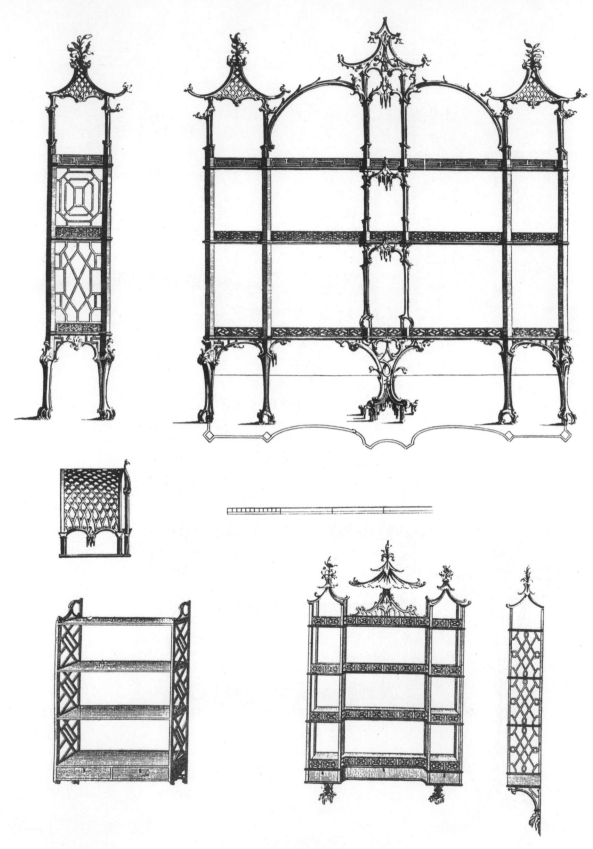

China Shelf and Hanging Shelves

CHIPPENDALE

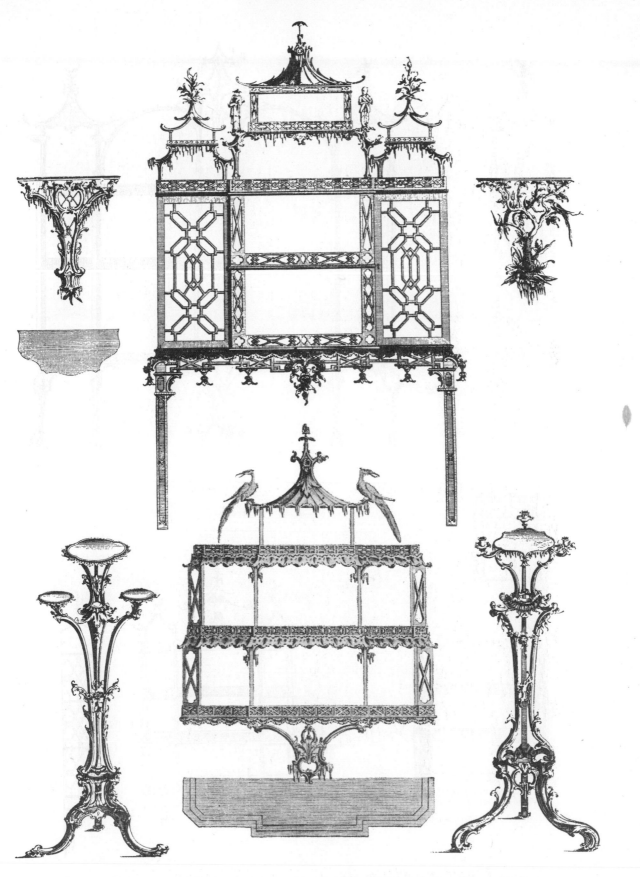

Brackets for Busts, China Shelves, Candle Stands, Hanging Shelves

CHIPPENDALE

Frames for Marble Slabs and French Commode Table

CHIPPENDALE

Gothic Clothes Chest and French Commode Table

CHIPPENDALE

French Commode Tables

CHIPPENDALE

French Commode Tables

CHIPPENDALE

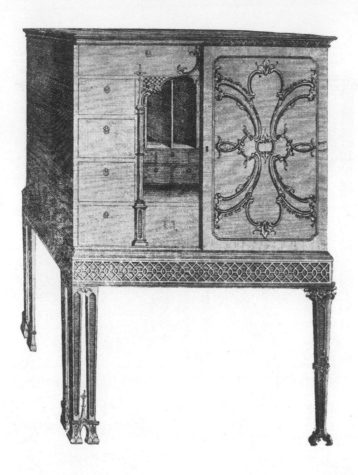

Cabinet and Frames for Marble Slabs

CHIPPENDALE

Commode Clothes Press, Clothes Chest, and Clothes Press

CHIPPENDALE

Two Designs for Clothes Chest, and Library Bookcase

CHIPPENDALE

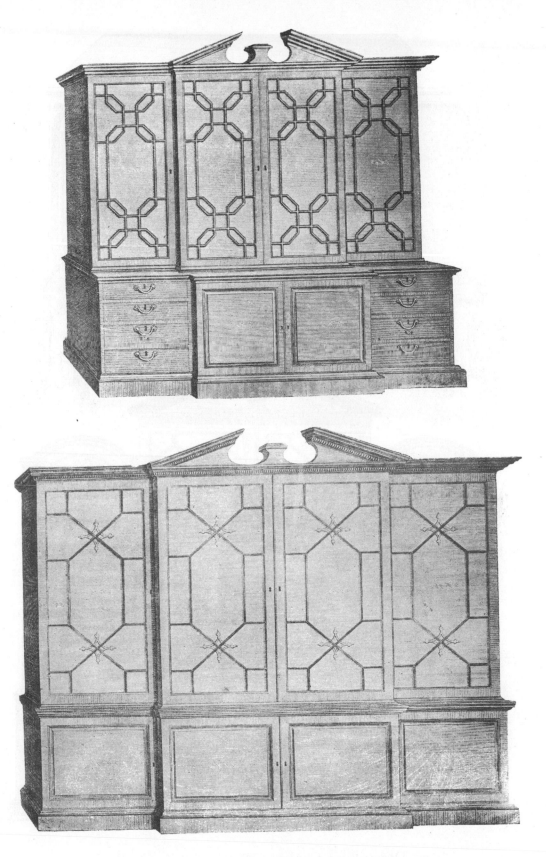

Library Bookcases

Library Bookcases

CHIPPENDALE

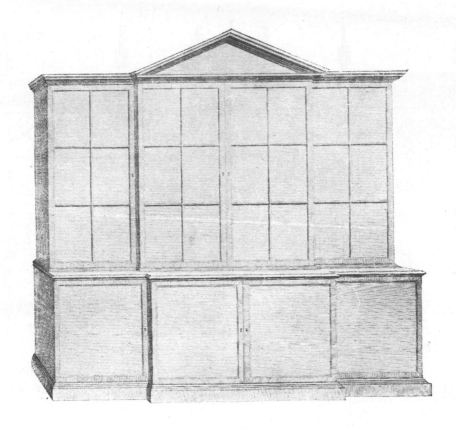

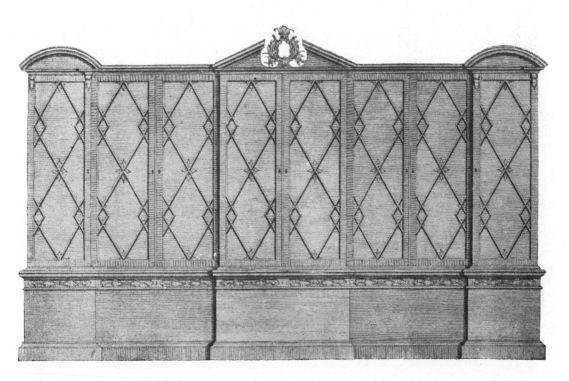

Library Bookcases

CHIPPENDALE

Writing Table and Library Bookcase

CHIPPENDALE

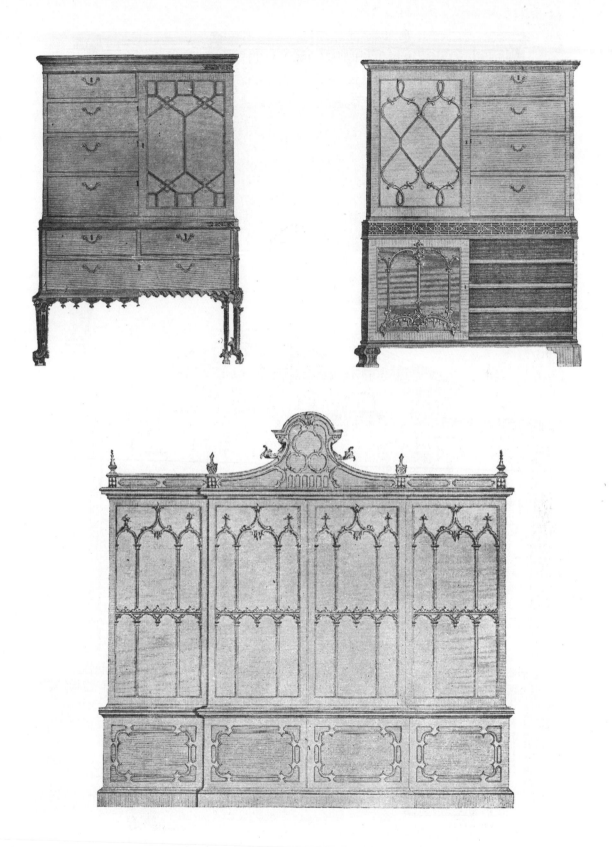

Two Chests of Drawers and Library Bookcase

CHIPPENDALE

Chest of Drawers, Clothes Press, China Case, and Frets

CHIPPENDALE

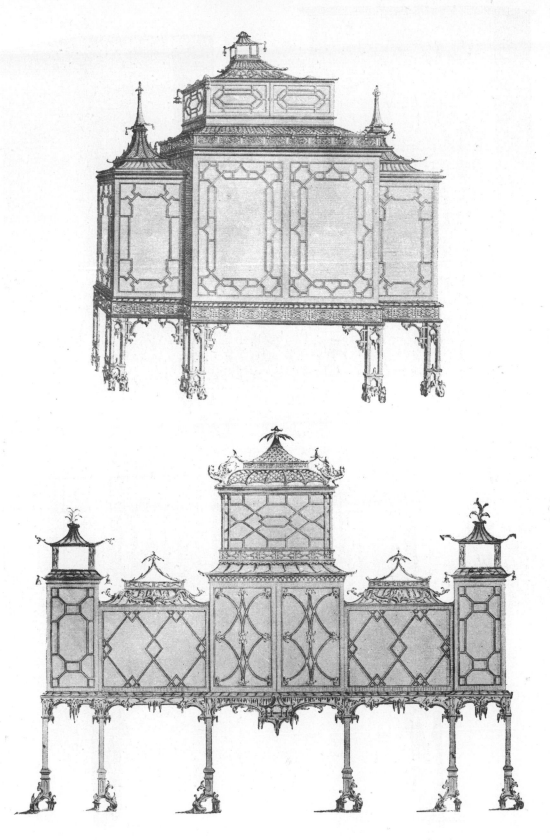

China Cases

CHIPPENDALE

Clothes Press

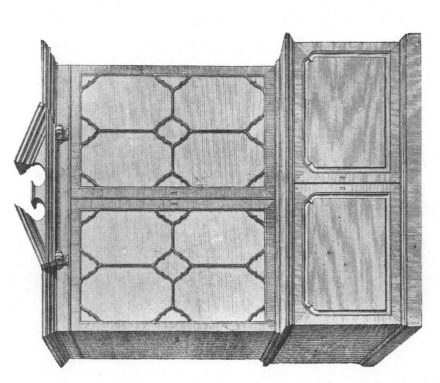

Library Bookcase

CHIPPENDALE

Gothic Cabinet

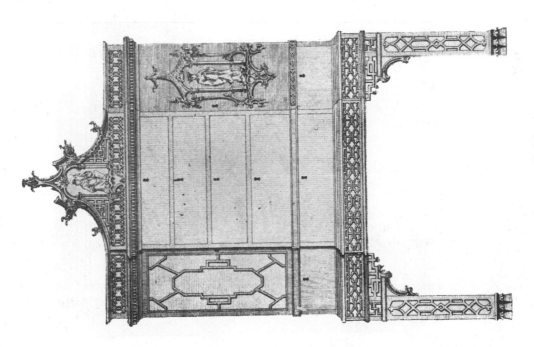

Chinese Cabinet

CHIPPENDALE

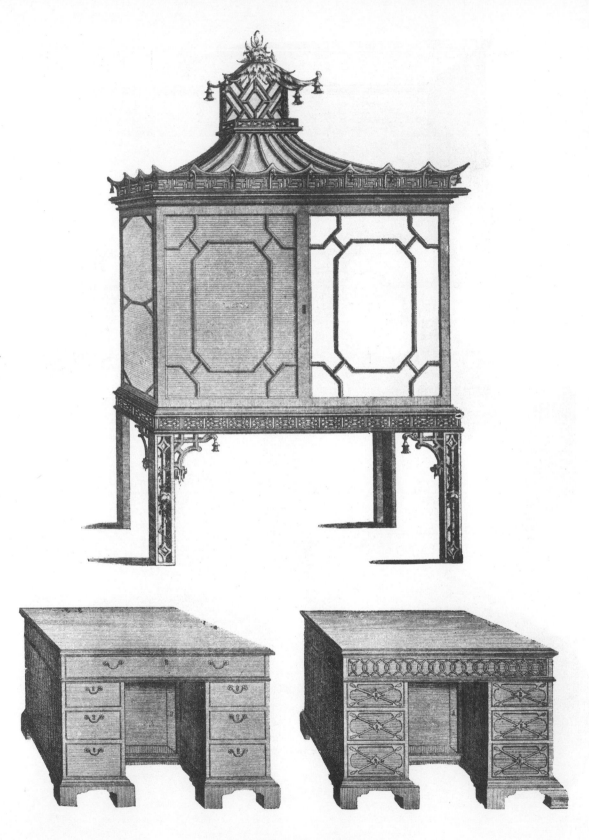

China and Bureau Tables

CHIPPENDALE

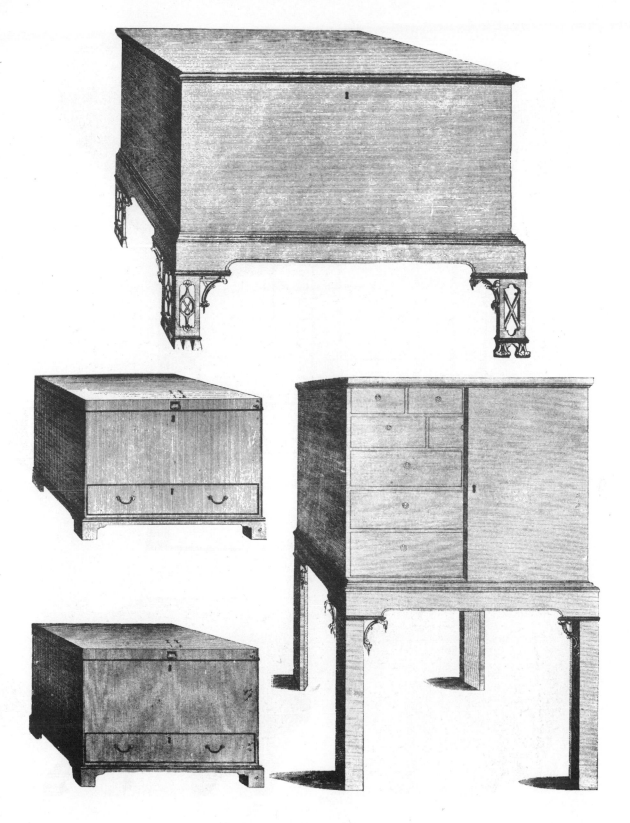

Clothes Chests and Cabinet

CHIPPENDALE

Clothes Chests and Library Tables

CHIPPENDALE

Library Tables

CHIPPENDALE

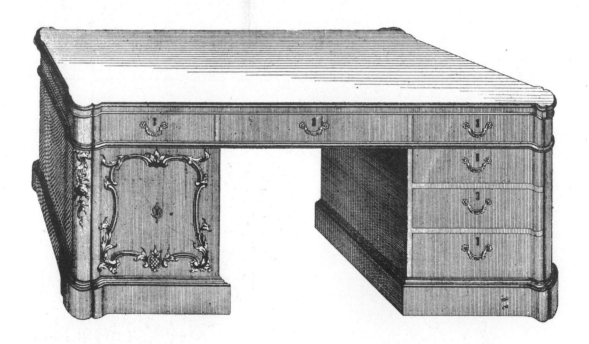

Library Tables

CHIPPENDALE

Dome Beds

CHIPPENDALE

Canopy Bed

CHIPPENDALE

Chinese Bed

CHIPPENDALE

Gothic Bed

CHIPPENDALE

Gothic Bed

CHIPPENDALE

Design for a Bed

CHIPPENDALE

Chinese Sofa

Chinese Sofa

THE CABINET-MAKER AND
UPHOLSTERER'S GUIDE

GEORGE HEPPLEWHITE

THOMAS CHIPPENDALE published his edition of the *Director* in 1754 and Thomas Sheraton published his first book of decorative designs in 1791. George Hepplewhite in point of time stands between the Chippendale and Sheraton periods, but his work undoubtedly is more akin to the Sheraton style. His individuality is becoming more recognised as time goes on, and as more scientific methods of criticism are applied to furniture by collectors. Hepplewhite designs as we know them were posthumous, for Hepplewhite died in 1786, and the cabinet-making business in Cripplegate was carried on by his widow, Alice, under the title of " A. Hepplewhite & Co." and the first edition of *The Cabinet-Maker and Upholsterer's Guide* appeared in 1788.

In dealing with Chippendale and with Sheraton there is in each case the personality of the man as a factor, and although little is known of the former there are many touches concerning the latter which give piquancy to his work. But of Hepplewhite, with his name frequently spelt, as in his signature to certain designs, " Heppelwhite," and coming into publicity under the sheltering title of a " Company," there is nothing known beyond his actual work.

Inheriting the traditions of Chippendale with his sound principles in regard to form and proportion, Hepplewhite belonged to the school of colourists of which Sheraton is the leading exponent. As a chair-maker he lacked the genius for symmetry which Chippendale possessed. Graceful and dainty as many of his chairs are they cannot compare with the finely balanced proportions of those of Chippendale. The Adam influence, with its severe lines and its cold chaste ornament, laid a hand on Hepplewhite, but his tendency always inclined to lightness and delicacy. Mahogany, of course, was the wood best adapted to the use of the chair-maker. His individuality is shown in characteristic variations from the Adam and the Chippendale style. He introduced, in or about 1770, oval and heart shaped backs disconnected with the seats ; and the honeysuckle, an adaptation of the Greek design acclimatised by Adam, the Prince of Wales' feathers, a frequent feature in his chair backs, and the wheat-ear, another of his patterns, indicate his original touch.

Some of his heart-back chairs have the Prince of Wales' feathers in strong bold carving as pronounced as those shown in the square-back chair illustrated (p. 13). This design was adopted by Hepplewhite when he made a set of chairs for George IV., then prince of Wales, and the style became the vogue from 1770 to 1780. In regard to the delicate carving of Hepplewhite of this pattern, and the wheat-ear and honeysuckle designs, they are of as deserved repute among connoisseurs as are the ribbon patterns of Chippendale. It is here that Hepplewhite holds his own as a carver, and it is a well-known fact to connoisseurs that the varieties of chairs of the Hepplewhite school exceed in number those of any other.

If Sheraton is *Louis Seize à l'Anglaise*, Hepplewhite represents the English interpretation of the classic revival which had originated in France. Robert Adam was the great high priest of this movement in England. He was the architect of the fine houses in the Adelphi, Bedford Square, Fitzroy Square, Manchester Square, Russell Square, Soho Square, Bryanston Square, Cumberland Place, etc., in London, and his work is to be seen to this day in Edinburgh, Glasgow, Bath, and in Dublin. From 1762 to 1792 the Adam influence was most pronounced in this country. The classical capitals, mouldings and shell flutings, and the light festoons and tracery in the Adam style, are welcome sights in many otherwise dreary streets in London. Robert Adam had brought from Italy the secret of making composition ornaments. It took the place of wood-carving in interior decoration and was far more durable than the plaster ornament which was then used on walls and ceilings.

Of his three brothers, James is best known, and together with him he produced in 1773 the first folio number of the celebrated Adam volumes on architecture. These volumes contained 125 plates, including the interiors of such mansions as Sion House, Caenwood, Lansdowne House and many others. Half of these plates consisted of designs for furniture, including cabinets, bureaus, candelabra, mirrors and other carved interior decoration.

Adam design was founded on different principles to the Chippendale school. Rococo ornament and massive breadth of carving, or intricate fretwork of Chinese origin, the fashions of Sir William Chambers and the absurdities of Kent, architect and general arbiter of taste, gave way to the classically correct translations of Adam, where furniture and interior decoration were treated as a whole. Architect though he was, no detail was too trivial for his attention. The pattern of the carpet or the design of the silver candelabra, the panel of the sideboard, or the decoration of the knife-case, each reflected the recurring ornament which was part of his scheme for the particular room.

Michael Angelo Pergolesi, who came to this country from Italy with Robert Adam, and who brought out *Designs for Various Ornaments*, with 70 plates, 1777-1801, folio, undoubtedly contributed, in conjunction with Adam, in founding the classical and Italian school of which Hepplewhite and Sheraton were the disciples. In regard to colour, Angelica Kauffmann, Cipriani and Zucchi were employed on painted panels and interior decorations by the brothers Adam. Painted chairs and "japanned" work were frequently made by Hepplewhite and his school. The surface was painted green, black, brown or buff, and a painted design in colours added. For instance beechwood, or even deal, was painted and many specimens exist belonging to this phase of his work, but as a rule time has dealt unkindly with this class of his furniture.

The oncoming of the satinwood period saw the further development of Hepplewhite designs in inlays of different coloured woods in table-tops, knife-boxes, or tea-caddies. The note of elegance began to become pronounced. A good deal of lathe work is noticeable in the tapering legs of chairs and tables and sideboards. Chippendale and his school were enamoured of solid and massive supports in the legs of cabriole form, but the straight slender leg was now the prevailing type, and under the guidance of Adam the arm of the chair takes a sudden curve downwards, and in satinwood examples this is a pronounced feature.

The tops for card-tables and dressing-tables and commodes as shown in the *Guide* exhibit the full play of fancy in his marqueterie. It is here that Hepplewhite departs most widely from the Chippendale school dependent for beauty on form. The carver was supplanted by the worker in marqueterie or by the painter.

But it must be remembered, and the fact comes with startling gravity, that Thomas Chippendale, in 1772, completed in co-operation with Robert Adam a magnificent inlaid writing-table for Harewood House, still in the possession of the Earl of Harewood. This sumptuous piece, rosewood inlaid with marqueterie of different coloured woods, and having bold pilasters headed by metal rams' heads with swags of fine cast and chased metal work, stands as a superbly beautiful piece of English inlaid furniture not surpassed by any other of the later schools. And Thomas Chippendale, master cabinetmaker, executed this. The original bill giving details and prices is in the possession of the Earl of Harewood, and is headed "Chippendale, Haig, and Co."

In the examination of Hepplewhite's designs certain of his *motifs* indicate their origin. The Side-table and Sideboard, on page 20, show in the serpentine front the direct influence of Adam. In some of Hepplewhite's chairs this front makes its appearance and the tapering and fluted legs have nothing in common with the school of Chippendale. The Pedestals and Vases and the Knife-cases (on pp. 22 and 23) are classic and architectural. The ingenuities and contrivances in some of the tables and minor pieces of furniture illustrated suggest the influence of Thomas Shearer, some of whose designs appear in the *Cabinet Makers*

London Book of Prices, and in *Designs for Household Furniture*, published in 1788. There is no doubt that Shearer exhibited an ingenuity in mechanical devices for folding furniture, for sliding shelves and drawers in useful furniture, which entitles him to recognition.

The details of Hepplewhite ornament will repay considerable study. The various intricate varieties of the shield-back chair, the delicate leaf-like decoration in the panels of bookcases, the extremely graceful adaptations of classic design in the *patera* on fronts of drawers and tables, and the dignity of much of the foliated design on panels and fronts is superlative. Compared with the Chippendale school the carving in mahogany is less robust, owing to the more slender surfaces on which Hepplewhite worked. To students the details of Hepplewhite must always appeal as of artistic excellence. His weakness as a designer chiefly lies in a certain want of homogeneity. His construction and cabinet work are careful and painstaking, but Hepplewhite as a whole never approached the ideal. He is great in parts.

ARTHUR HAYDEN.

THE
CABINET-MAKER
AND
UPHOLSTERER's GUIDE;

OR,

REPOSITORY OF DESIGNS

FOR EVERY ARTICLE OF

HOUSEHOLD FURNITURE,

IN THE NEWEST AND MOST APPROVED TASTE:

DISPLAYING

A GREAT VARIETY OF PATTERNS FOR

Chairs	Tea Caddies	Hanging Shelves
Stools	Tea Trays	Fire Screens
Sofas	Card Tables	Beds
Confidante	Pier Tables	Field Beds
Ducheffe	Pembroke Tables	Sweep Tops for Ditto
Side Boards	Tambour Tables	Bed Pillars
Pedeftals and Vafes	Dreffing Glaffes	Candle Stands
Cellerets	Dreffing Tables and Drawers	Lamps
Knife-Cafes	Commodes	Pier Glaffes
Defk and Book-Cafes	Rudd's Table	Terms for Bufts
Secretary and Book Cafes	Bidets	Cornices for Library
Library Cafes	Night Tables	Cafes, Wardrobes, &c. at large
Library Tables	Bafon Stands	Ornamented Tops for Pier
Reading Defks	Wardrobes	Tables, Pembroke Tables,
Chefts of Drawers	Pot Cupboards	Commodes, &c. &c.
Urn Stands	Brackets	

In the PLAINEST and moft ENRICHED STYLES; with a SCALE to each,
and an EXPLANATION in LETTER PRESS.

ALSO

THE PLAN OF A ROOM,

SHEWING THE PROPER DISTRIBUTION OF THE FURNITURE.

The Whole exhibiting near THREE HUNDRED different DESIGNS, engraved
on ONE HUNDRED and TWENTY-EIGHT PLATES:

FROM DRAWINGS

By A. HEPPLEWHITE and Co. CABINET-MAKERS.

THE THIRD EDITION, IMPROVED.

LONDON:

Publifhed by I. and J. TAYLOR, at the ARCHITECTURAL LIBRARY,
No. 56, HOLBORN, oppofite GREAT TURN-STILE.
MDCCXCIV.

PREFACE

TO unite elegance and utility, and blend the useful with the agreeable, has ever been considered a difficult, but an honourable task. How far we have succeeded in the following work it becomes us not to say, but rather to leave it, with all due deference, to the determination of the Public at large.

It may be allowable to say, we have exerted our utmost endeavour to produce a work which shall be useful to the mechanic and serviceable to the gentleman. With this view, after having fixed upon such articles as were necessary to a complete suit of Furniture, our judgment was called forth in selecting such patterns as were most likely to be of general use—in choosing such points of view as would show them most distinctly—and in exhibiting such fashions as were necessary to answer the end proposed, and convey a just idea of English taste in furniture for houses.

English taste and workmanship have, of late years, been much sought for by surrounding nations; and the mutibility of all things, but more especially of fashions, has rendered the labours of our predecessors in this line of little use; nay, at this day, they can only tend to mislead those Foreigners who seek a knowledge of English taste in the various articles of household furniture.

The same reason, in favour of this work, will apply also to many of our own Countrymen and Artizans, whose distance from the metropolis makes even an imperfect knowledge of its improvements acquired with much trouble and expense. Our labours will, we hope, tend to remove the difficulty; and as our idea of the useful was such articles as are generally serviceable in genteel life, we flatter ourselves the labour and pains we have bestowed on this work will not be considered as time uselessly spent.

To Residents in London, though our drawings are all new, yet, as we designedly followed the latest or most prevailing fashion only, purposely omitting such articles, whose recommendation was mere novelty, and perhaps a violation of all established rule, the production of whim, at the instance of caprice, whose appetite must ever suffer disappointment if any similar thing had been previously thought of; we say, having regularly avoided those fancies, and steadily adhered to such articles only as are of general use and service, one principal hope for favour and encouragement will be, in having combined near three hundred different patterns for furniture in so small a space, and at so small a price. In this instance we hope for reward; and though we lay no claim to extraordinary merit in our designs, we flatter ourselves they will be found serviceable to young workmen in general, and occasionally to more experienced ones.

CONTENTS

HEPPLEWHITE

THE CABINET-MAKER AND UPHOLSTERER'S GUIDE

HEPPLEWHITE

Pembroke Tables and Tea Trays

HEPPLEWHITE

Tops for Card Tables and Pier Tables

Tops for Pier Tables and Tea Chests

Tops for Pembroke Tables, Pier Table, and Tea Caddies

HEPPLEWHITE

Tops for Dressing Tables and Commodes, and Pier Table

HEPPLEWHITE

Card Tables and Library Case showing end view

HEPPLEWHITE

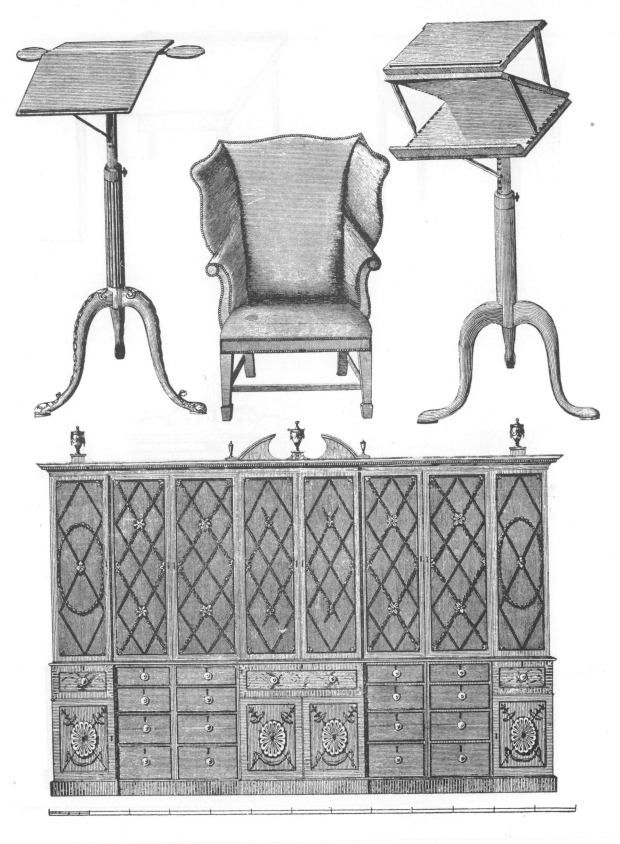

Reading Desks, Easy Chair, and Library Case

HEPPLEWHITE

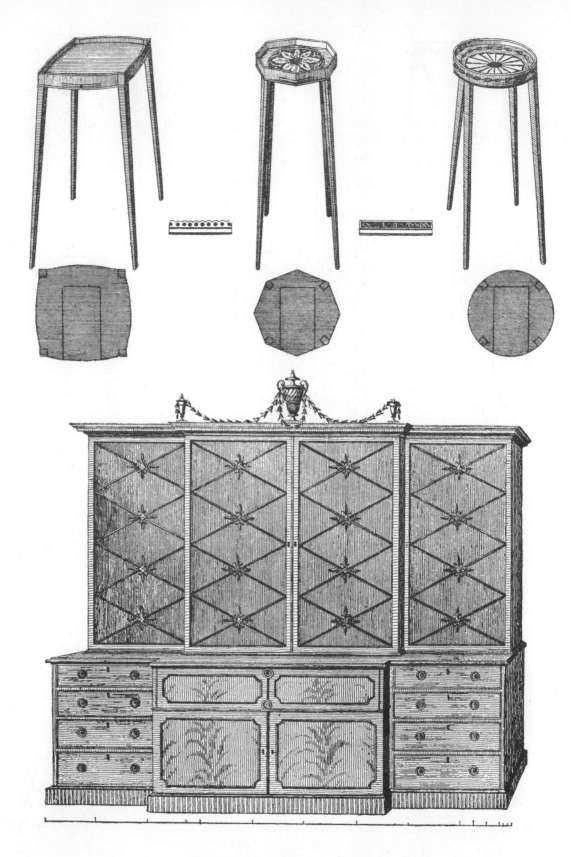

Urn Stands and Library Case

HEPPLEWHITE

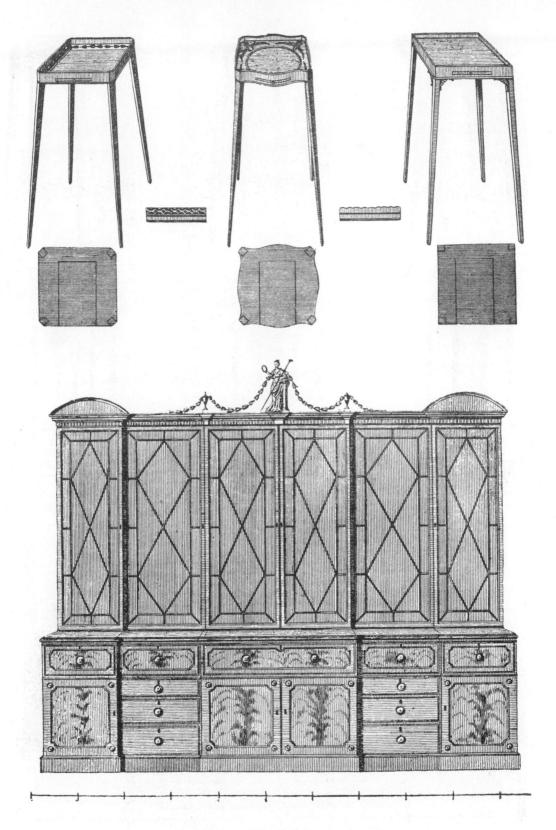

Urn Stands and Library Case

HEPPLEWHITE

Chairs

HEPPLEWHITE

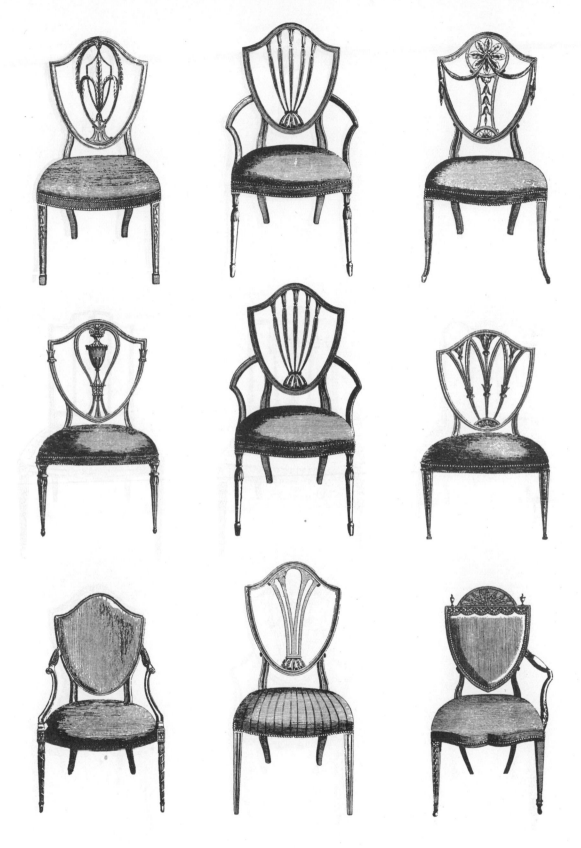

Chairs

HEPPLEWHITE

Chairs

HEPPLEWHITE

Designs for Chair Backs

HEPPLEWHITE

Window Seats and Stools

HEPPLEWHITE

Window Seats and Stool, and Gouty Stool

HEPPLEWHITE

Duchesse and Confidante

HEPPLEWHITE

Bar-back Sofa, and Sofa

HEPPLEWHITE

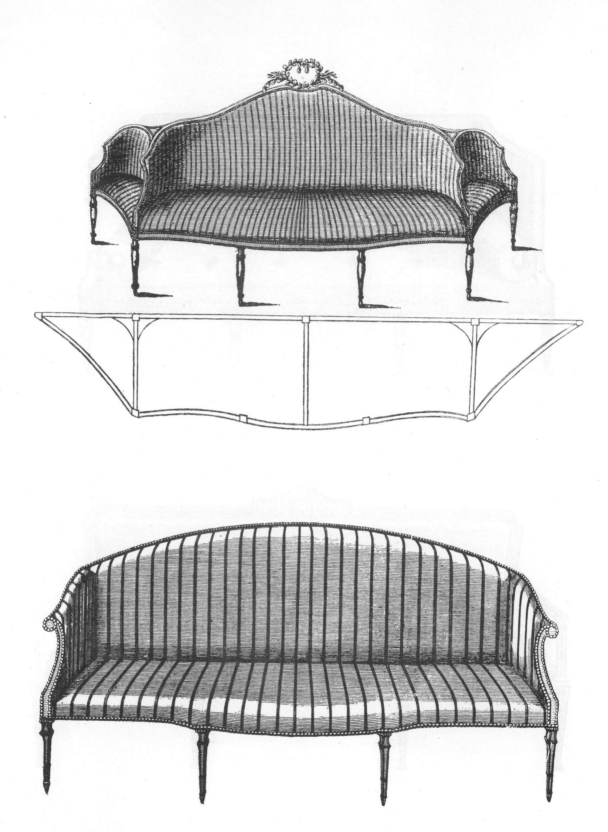

Confidante and Sofa

HEPPLEWHITE

Sofas

HEPPLEWHITE

Side Table and Sideboard

HEPPLEWHITE

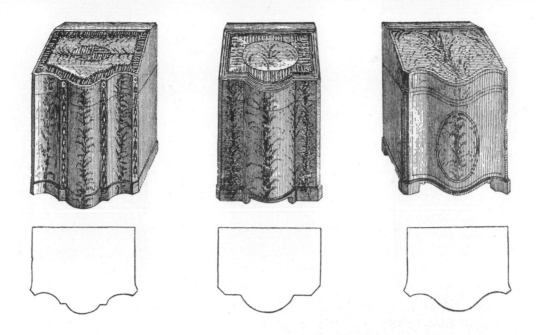

Knife Cases and Sideboard

HEPPLEWHITE

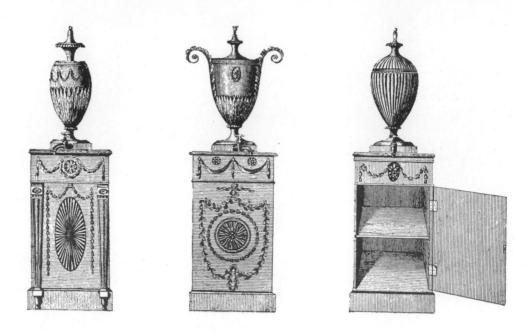

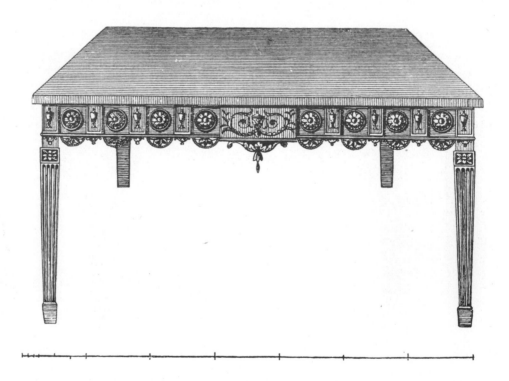

Pedestals and Vases, and Side Table

HEPPLEWHITE

Knife Cases and Side Table

HEPPLEWHITE

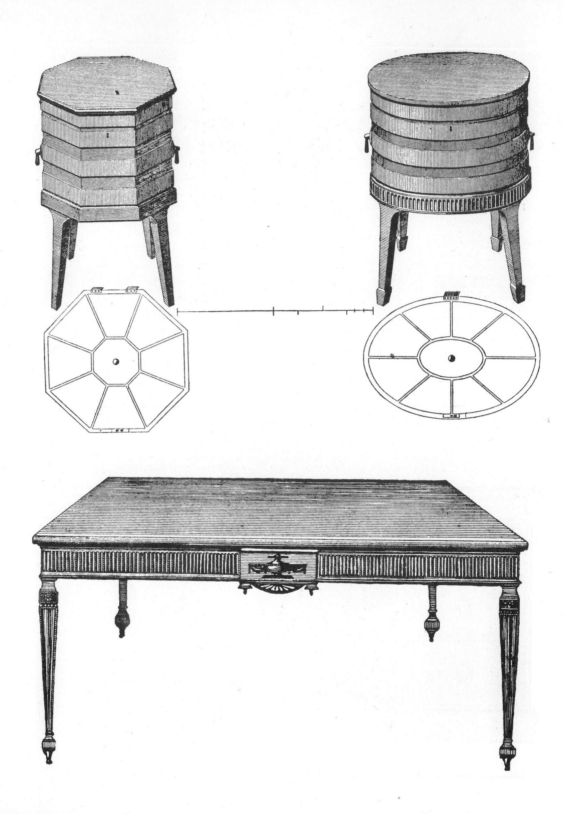

Cellarets and Side Table

HEPPLEWHITE

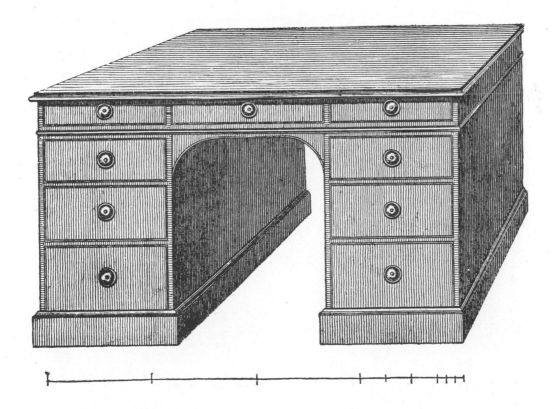

Pedestals and Vases, and Library Table

HEPPLEWHITE

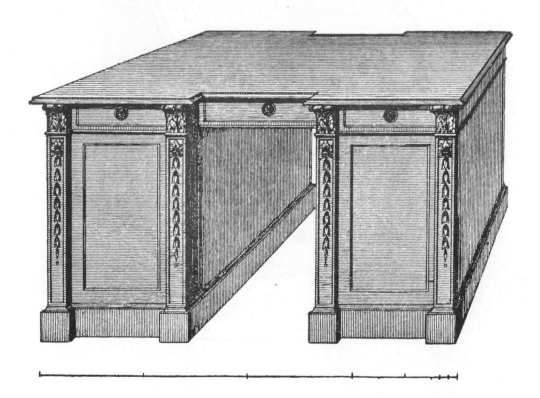

Library Tables

HEPPLEWHITE

Desk and Bookcase

HEPPLEWHITE

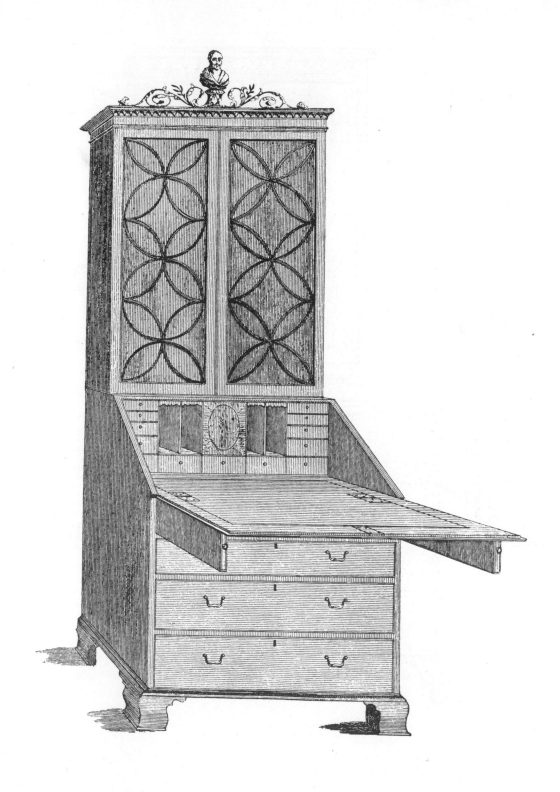

Desk and Bookcase

HEPPLEWHITE

Secretary and Bookcase

HEPPLEWHITE

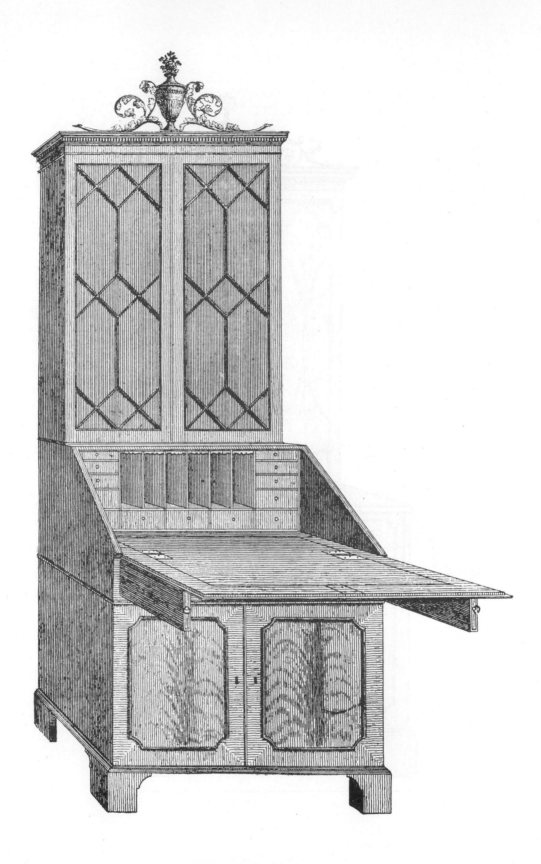

Desk and Bookcase

HEPPLEWHITE

Secretary and Bookcase

HEPPLEWHITE

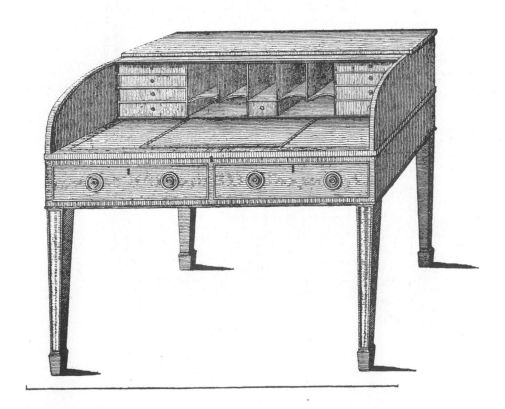

Tambour Writing Tables

HEPPLEWHITE

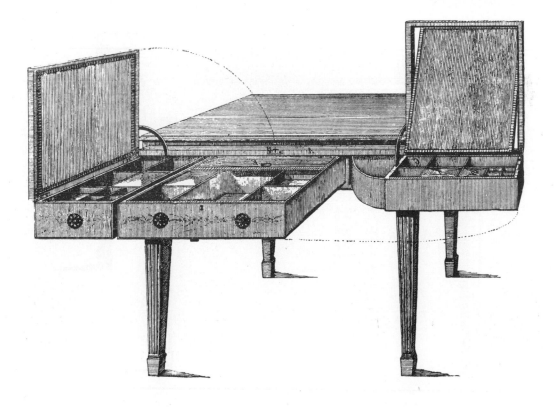

Hanging Shelves, and Rudd's Table

HEPPLEWHITE

Terms for Busts, etc.

HEPPLEWHITE

Lamps and Wardrobe

HEPPLEWHITE

Wardrobe

HEPPLEWHITE

Wardrobe

HEPPLEWHITE

Double Chest of Drawers

HEPPLEWHITE

Double Chest of Drawers

Chests of Drawers

HEPPLEWHITE

Dressing Drawers and Commode

HEPPLEWHITE

Shaving Tables, Bidet Shaving Table, and Commode Dressing Table

HEPPLEWHITE

Night Tables and Dressing Drawers

HEPPLEWHITE

Dressing Glasses and Dressing Drawers

HEPPLEWHITE

Pole Fire-Screens and Dressing Drawers

HEPPLEWHITE

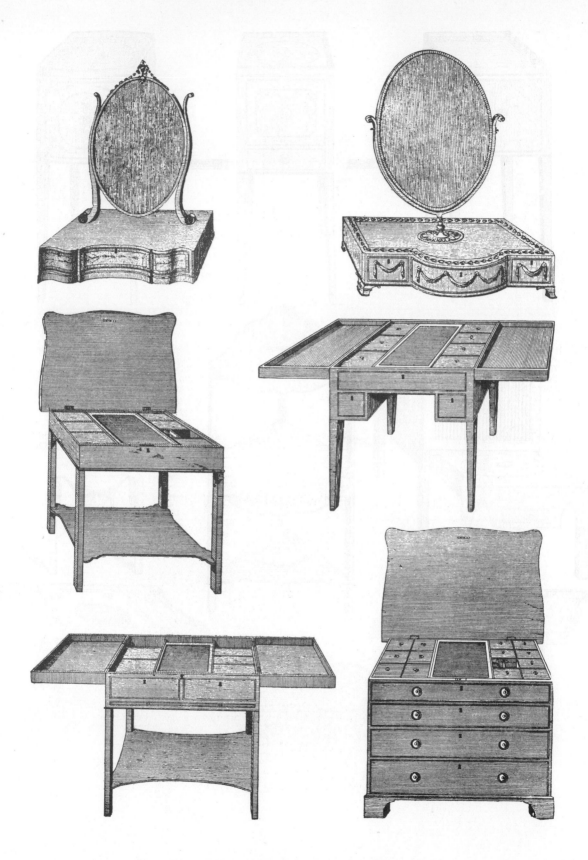

Dressing Glasses, and Ladies' Dressing Tables

HEPPLEWHITE

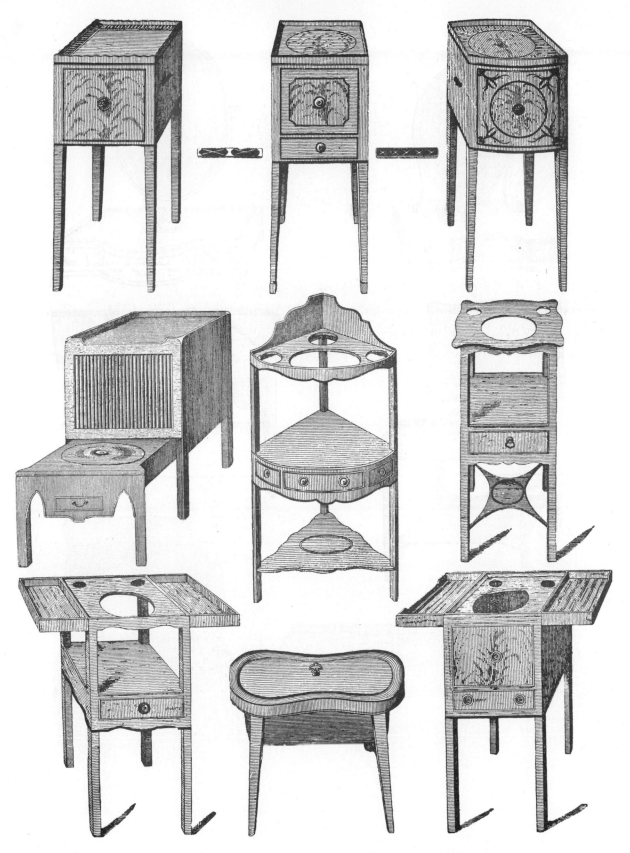

Pot Cupboards, Night Table, Basin Stands, and Bidet

HEPPLEWHITE

Cornices for Beds or Windows, and Girandoles

HEPPLEWHITE

Cornices for Beds or Windows, and Hanging Lamps

HEPPLEWHITE

Girandoles and Pier Glasses

Cornice for Bed or Window, Girandoles, and Horse Fire-Screens

Pier Glasses

HEPPLEWHITE

Cornices and Base Mouldings

HEPPLEWHITE

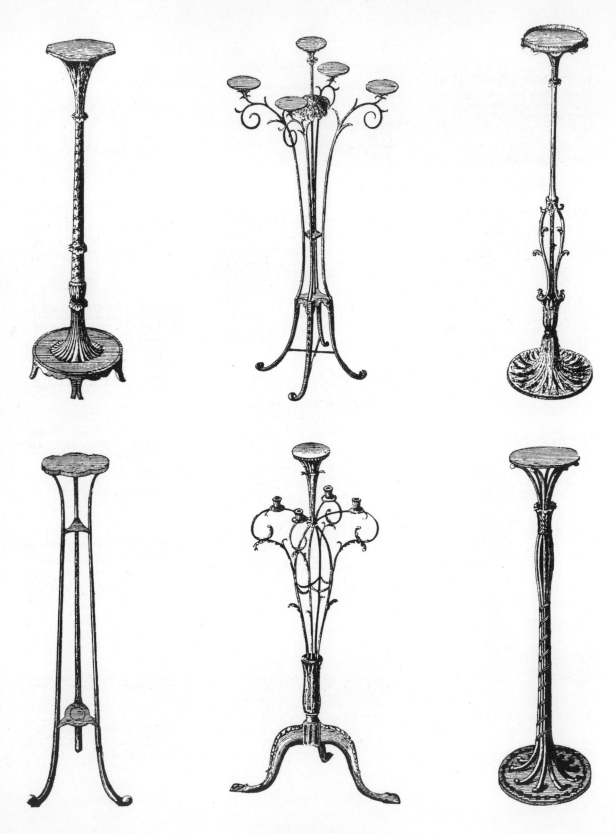

Candle Stands

HEPPLEWHITE

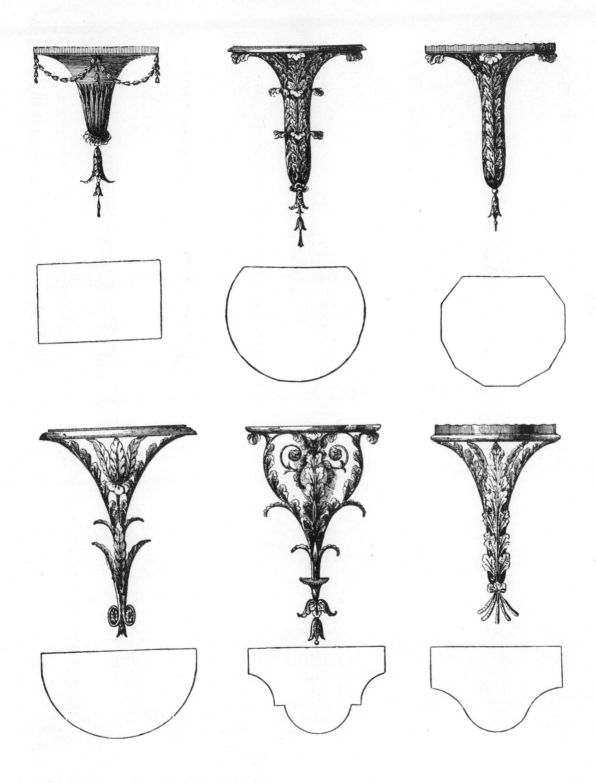

Brackets

HEPPLEWHITE

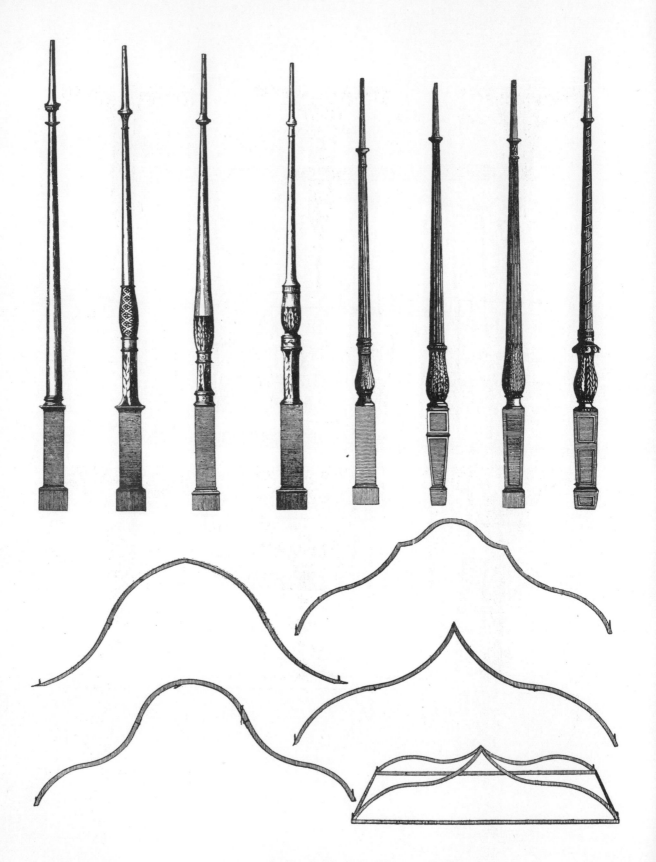

Bed Pillars and Sweeps for Field Bed Tops

HEPPLEWHITE

Design for a Bed

HEPPLEWHITE

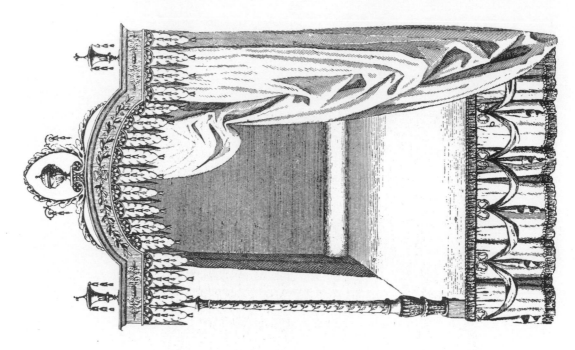

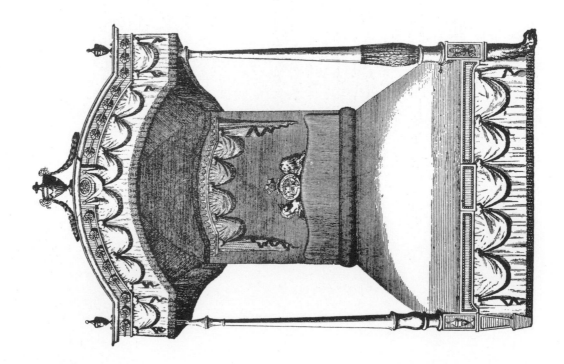

Designs for Beds

HEPPLEWHITE

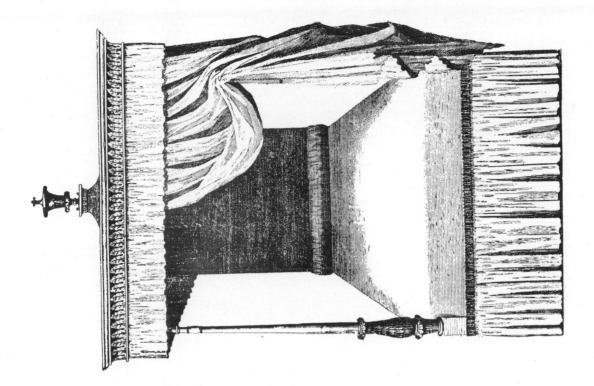

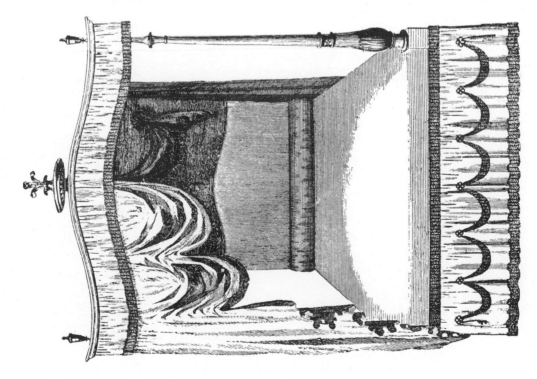

Designs for Beds

THE CABINET-MAKER AND
UPHOLSTERER'S DRAWING-BOOK

THOMAS SHERATON

1751-1804

IN Chippendale and Hepplewhite two types of master cabinet-makers and designers are exemplified. Both were practical craftsmen and successful business men. Robert Adam, the architect, and Thomas Sheraton the visionary, are representative of designers who influenced their contemporaries in a most remarkable degree, but who did not actually practise the art of cabinet-making themselves. (Sheraton abandoned practical work in 1793.) But here the comparison between Adam and Sheraton ends, for the former was the leading spirit in a great movement which had far-reaching effects in establishing a style which permeated architectural design and interior decoration and furniture. Robert Adam was eminently successful, but unfortunately Thomas Sheraton was one of life's failures, and died in poverty.

Born at Stockton-on-Tees in 1751, Sheraton describes himself as a "mechanic," in a religious pamphlet he published at Stockton in 1782. He came to London as a journeyman cabinet-maker in 1790, and after a few years he ceased working at the bench and occupied a small stationer's shop, where he was author, publisher, bookseller, teacher of drawing, and an occasional preacher at Baptist chapels. His character resembles that of William Blake, the painter, poet, and engraver, his contemporary. The successful Fuseli said of Blake's designs that they were "damned good to steal from," and there is little doubt that Sheraton's designs, published and unpublished, were a fine quarry for more practical men with greater aptitude for business. His own words convey a touch of his philosophic quality when he describes himself as "employed in racking my invention to design fine and pleasing cabinet-work. I can be well content to sit on a wooden bottom chair myself, provided I can but have common food and raiment wherewith to pass through life in peace."

It is the irony of fate that for the contemporary satin-wood furniture of Sheraton design, instinct with refined beauty, and graceful with a rare delicacy of invention, sensational prices are reached in the auction-room. Here again he touches William Blake, whose designs have won him eternal fame, but who often had not money enough when he lived to buy copper-plates to record his visions.

Another picture of the man Sheraton with his wife and two children has been given to posterity by Adam Black who, in 1804, came to London from Edinburgh in search of work. It was the year of Sheraton's death. Young Black found him " in an obscure street, his house, half shop half dwelling house, and looked himself like a worn-out Methodist minister, with threadbare black coat. I took tea with them one afternoon. There were a cup and saucer for the host, and another for his wife, and a little porringer for their daughter. The wife's cup and saucer were given to me, and she had to put up with a little porringer." The young Scotsman, afterwards publisher of the *Encyclopædia Britannica*, received half a guinea for his week's work in trying to bring arrangement into the ill-kept shop. " Miserable as the pay was," he writes, " I was half ashamed to take it from the poor man."[1]

Sheraton's first book of designs was issued in quarto parts, 1791-1794, " The Cabinet-Maker and Upholsterer's Drawing-Book." The complete volume is in three parts, together with an *Appendix* and an *Accompaniment*, containing a " variety of ornament adapted to the cabinet and chair branches." This consists of 113 plates of articles of furniture, sides of rooms, &c. The third edition of the *Drawing-Book* in four parts was published in 1802, and contains 122 plates, which edition is here republished. After Sheraton's death there appeared in 1812 a series of designs which Sheraton had in hand for publication. This " Designs for Household Furniture," with 84 plates " by the late T. Sheraton, Cabinet-Maker," is here republished.

The latter half of the eighteenth century from 1748, when Ince and Mayhew produced their volume with three hundred designs for *Household Furniture*, down to the death of Sheraton, was most prolific in the publication of illustrated books of design. The bibliography of the subject is full, and there is ample evidence that in the closing years of the century there was a complexity of theory. Styles of one maker were readily adapted by another, and published designs of men related to each other in details of construction, and deriving inspiration from a common source, overlapped in point of time. The number of master cabinet-makers, upholsterers, and chair-makers given by Sheraton as working in London and the vicinity was no less than 252. There is no doubt that many of these men did good work. What is known, for instance, of Seddon, " one of the most eminent cabinet-makers in London"? But according to the *Annual Register* of 1768 he had a fire at his premises in Aldersgate Street which did damage to the extent of £20,000.

The early Chippendale school had given place to the school of mar-

[1] " Memoirs of Adam Black," 1885.

queterie workers, compeers of Hepplewhite, who employed satin-wood veneer and inlays of coloured woods, and who revelled in painted panels with subjects as French in feeling as the lunettes of Natoire and Boucher. In 1773, so strongly had the current set in for colour, that Chippendale, then an old man, made a set of satin-wood furniture after the designs of Robert Adam for the Lascelles family. The beautiful contrasts of colour against the golden satin-wood ground are remarkable. The dressing-table commode of this suite has a veneered satin-wood ground inlaid with green garrya husks, and wreaths of this inlay encircle panels of seated figures of Diana and Minerva inlaid with coloured woods and ivory on a black ground. So elaborate were some of the pieces of this suite at Harewood House that the cast and chased metal work equals that of *Gouthière*.

Prior to Sheraton's day pieces of lesser magnificence than those executed for noblemen's mansions were painted in the Hepplewhite style, and the use of satin-wood was becoming popular. Sheraton came to London in 1790, and died in 1804, so that his influence as a designer extended only over a period of fourteen years. He found a rapidly increasing love for the elegance of the French designers, and he identified himself so much with boudoir art that many of his designs might well be taken as original French conceptions. The lathe is used more freely in Sheraton chairs and tables than by his forerunners. His details have a charm and delicacy unsurpassed in English design. In comparison with Hepplewhite he had a finely developed sense of proportion. Grace and symmetry are never wanting in his designs. He held very sound views in regard to ornament which in his work was never meaningless. It is part of the construction, and never appears to be an afterthought. It is reticent and subdued, but possesses a beauty which successive generations of connoisseurs have acclaimed.

The *Drawing-Book* tells its own story. The "Conversation Chairs" and Sofa (p. 3) require a word of explanation. The chairs were used by gentlemen who sat astride with the back of the chair facing the sofa, the seat of honour. The top of the chair was used for leaning upon. The backs for Parlour Chairs (p. 4) exhibit a rare delicacy of finely proportioned ornament. The delicacy of detail is exemplified in the Elbows for Drawing-Room Chairs (p. 7), and the Chair Legs (p. 8) indicate something more detailed in carving than is usually associated with Sheraton by collectors and students familiar only with the satin-wood examples of table legs of tapering form, with no carving, but dependent on inlay for their decoration. In the Card Tables and the Kidney Table (p. 13), one sees at once the touch of Sheraton. Chippendale would not have produced such a design as the kidney table with its novel form and its bowed fronts, and slender grace and elegance. Hepplewhite was too studied and painstaking to have conceived so original a design. Similarly in the borders for Pier Tables, Sheraton is as bold and original in his marqueterie design as was Chippendale in his carving in mahogany.

In regard to the elaborate mechanical devices in dressing tables and library furniture, it is possible that Shearer, who was a past master in such inventions, may have followed out these designs of Sheraton, and he probably had an influence on Sheraton in their conception.

The painted panel of the Hepplewhite school found its ideal in such examples as the Ornament for a Table (p. 14) with the fine figures of Venus and Adonis.

In regard to the painting of Sheraton's furniture by Angelica Kaufmann, there is room for considerable scepticism, as Sheraton did not come to London till 1790, and Angelica, on her marriage with Zucchi, left England in 1781, and resided in Rome till 1795.

A series of Bookcase Doors (pp. 20 and 21) exhibits Sheraton's originality of idea, and the leaves in carving show a grace and firmness of touch unapproached by Hepplewhite in his Prince of Wales's feathers.

The "Horse Dressing Glass" (p. 32) still retained in the word "Cheval" is merely a term denoting a larger size, made familiar in such phrases as horse-play, horse-laugh, horse-chestnut.

The Sideboard and Sideboard Table (p. 34) show graceful lines and curves not before introduced into English furniture, and essentially belonging to the school of designers founded by Sheraton.

In the *Designs for Household Furniture* the chairs depart in marked manner from the grace and symmetry of Sheraton's earlier forms. They mark his decadent period when he came under the influence of the Napoleonic modes in French furniture, and they betray, what is rare in Sheraton, a slight want of balance. Some of his Library Tables (notably that illustrated, p. 94) exhibit powerful design and well-balanced proportions.

As a summary of Sheraton's style, it may be advanced that he imparted to furniture a subtlety and elegance which broke away from the old traditions of the school of carvers. Robert Adam regarded furniture as an adjunct to his architectural details. He made the lines of his furniture designs subservient to the scheme of decoration. Away from its environment Adam furniture is hard and lacks repose. Sheraton designed furniture for the love of his art. His style is rich with piquant suggestiveness. In colour it is alluring, in form it is elegant and refined, and full of artistic surprises. The dainty boudoir was his by conquest. His furniture belongs to the age of the insipidities of the Bartolozzi school of stipple engraving, and to the finnicking mannerisms of the days of colour prints. His colour schemes found favour with Mrs Siddons, Mrs Fitzherbert, and Lady Hamilton. His importations from France, the pseudo-classicism of the court of Marie Antoinette, took root here as something new. But in spite of the source of his inspiration there is an originality of treatment which marks his style as distinctive, and stamps Sheraton as a master designer. There is much which may some day be discovered by research relating to firms such as Gillow and others, for whom Sheraton designed ; at present his work for contemporary cabinet-makers is lost in a crowded and prolific period. One is on sure ground when studying his published books of designs. Beyond this Sheraton's actual work is largely conjectural. But his influence in English furniture design is permanent.

ARTHUR HAYDEN.

THE
CABINET-MAKER
AND
UPHOLSTERER'S
DRAWING-BOOK.

IN FOUR PARTS.

BY
THOMAS SHERATON.
CABINET-MAKER.

=============

Recommended by many Workmen of the First Abilities in London
who have themselves inspected the Work.

THE THIRD EDITION REVISED,
And the whole Embellished with 122 Elegant Copper-Plates.

——————

LONDON:
PRINTED BY T. BENSLEY, BOLT COURT, FLEET STREET,
FOR W. BAYNES (SUCCESSOR TO G. TERRY), 54, PATERNOSTER ROW.
SOLD ALSO BY J. ARCHER, DUBLIN, AND ALL OTHER BOOKSELLERS.

———

1802

To

Cabinet-Makers and Upholsterers

IN GENERAL

Gentlemen,

I presume that to publish a Drawing-book answerable to the preceding title page will not require many words to convince you either of the necessity or propriety of the attempt.

Nor will it be requisite to use an ostentatious preface to recommend it to your notice, or to persuade you of the utility of such an undertaking. Therefore, what I have further to say in this Address shall be to give some account of my plan, and point out to you the difference between this and other books which have been published for the assistance and use of Cabinet-makers and Upholsterers.

Books of various designs in cabinet work, ornamented according to the taste of the times in which they were published, have already appeared. But none of these, as far as I know, profess to give any instructions relative to the art of making perspective drawings, or to treat of such geometrical lines as ought to be known by persons of both professions, especially such of them as have a number of men under their direction. Nor have these books given accurate patterns at large for ornaments to enrich and embellish the various pieces of work which frequently occur in the cabinet branch. Such patterns are also highly necessary to copy from by those who would sufficiently qualify themselves for giving a good sketch, or regular drawing, of anything they meet with, or are required to draw for others. Nor indeed would this performance answer so well to the title of a Drawing-book without them. I hope, therefore, that in some degree the above defect is supplied in the following work, and that it will be considered as an enhancement to the real value and usefulness of the Cabinet-Maker and Upholsterer's Drawing-Book to be furnished with a variety of such ornaments as shall serve, both for the purpose of the learner, and also to assist the ideas of those who have occasion to adorn their work in this way.

As I have alluded to some books of designs, it may be proper here just to say something of them. I have seen one which seems to have been published before Chippendale's. I infer this from the antique appearance of the furniture, for there is no date to it; but the title informs us that it was composed by a Society of Cabinet-makers in London. It gives no instructions for drawing in any form, but we may venture to say that those who drew the designs wanted a good share of teaching themselves.

Chippendale's book seems to be next in order to this, but the former is without comparison to it, either as to size or real merit. Chippendale's book has, it is true, given us the proportions of the Five Orders, and lines for two or three cases, which is all it pretends to relative to rules for drawing: and, as for the designs themselves, they are now wholly antiquated and laid aside, though possessed of great merit, according to the times in which they were executed. But it may here be remarked to his credit, that although he has not given rules for drawing in[1] perspective himself yet he was sensible of their importance, and use in designing, and therefore he says in his preface: "Without some knowledge of the rules of perspective, the cabinet-maker cannot make the designs of his work intelligible, nor shew, in a little compass, the whole conduct and effect of the piece. These, therefore, referring to architecture also, ought to be carefully studied by every one who would excel in this branch, since they are the very soul and basis of his art."

After Chippendale's work there appeared, in the year sixty-five, a book of designs for chairs only, though it is called "The Cabinet-Maker's real Friend and Companion," as well as the Chairmaker's. This publication professes to shew their method of striking out all kinds of bevel-work, by which, as the author says, the most ignorant person will be immediately acquainted with what many artists have served seven years to know. But this assertion both exceeds the bounds of modesty and truth, since there is nothing in his directions for bevel-work, which he parades so much about, but what an apprentice boy may be taught by seven hours' proper instructions. With respect to the geometrical view of the Five Orders which he has given, these are useful, and the only thing in his book which at this day is worthy notice; as all his chairs are nearly as old as Chippendale's, and seem to be copied from them.

The succeeding publication to this seems to be Ince's and Mayhew's Book of Designs in Cabinet and Chair Work, with three plates, containing some examples of foliage ornaments, intended for the young designer to copy from, but which can be of no service to any learner now, as they are

---

[1] This is strictly true of the third edition of Chippendale's book · but the first edition of it, printed in 1754, has given two chairs, a dressing-table, and a book-case in perspective, shewing the lines for drawing them. But why these examples were not continued in the succeeding editions I know not. In the last edition of any work, we naturally expect to see it in its best state, having received its last revisal from the author, or some other hand equal to the task; and therefore it can never be thought unfair for a reader to form his judgment of a book from the last impression. I hope, therefore, this will sufficiently apologise for the above observation.

such kind of ornaments as are wholly laid aside in the cabinet branch, according to the present taste.

The designs in cabinets and chairs are, of course, of the same cast, and therefore have suffered the same fate. Yet, in justice to the work, it may be said to have been a book of merit in its day, though much inferior to Chippendale's, which was a real original, as well as more extensive and masterly in its designs.

In looking over Ince's book I observed two card-tables with some perspective lines, shewing the manner of designing them. These, so far as they go, are a useful attempt; but certain it is to me, from some experience in teaching, that no person can have the smallest acquaintance with the principles of perspective, merely from seeing two or three lines joined to a plate, without proper instructions by letter-press. It is true, a description is given of these lines in the 7th page of his book, but not equal to what is absolutely requisite to such as have no previous acquaintance with the art; and those that have, will not require that which can give them no assistance. Properly speaking then, what is done in this book, relative to perspective lines, can only serve as a hint to the workman, that this art is essential in designing.

In the year 1788 was published, "The Cabinet-maker's and Up-holsterer's Guide," in which are found no directions for drawing in any form, nor any pretensions to it. The whole merit of the performance rests on the designs, with a short description to each plate prefixed. Some of these designs are not without merit, though it is evident that the perspective is, in some instances, erroneous. But, notwithstanding the late date of Hepplewhite's book, if we compare some of the designs, particularly the chairs, with the newest taste, we shall find that this work has already caught the decline, and, perhaps, in a little time will suddenly die in the disorder. This instance may serve to convince us of that fate which all books of the same kind will ever be subject to. Yet it must be owned, that books of this sort have their usefulness for a time; and, when through change of fashions they are become obsolete, they serve to shew the taste of former ages.

I shall now conclude this account of books of designs with observing, that in the same year was given a quarto book of different pieces of furniture, with the Cabinet-maker's London Book of Prices; and, consider-ing that it did not make its appearance under the title of a Book of Designs, but only to illustrate the prices, it certainly lays claim to merit, and does honour to the publishers.

Upon the whole then, if the intended publication, which now petitions your patronage and support, be so compiled and composed as fully to answer, and also to merit, the title which has been given to it, I think it will be found greatly to supply the defects of those books now mentioned, and will appear to be on as lasting a foundation as can well be expected in a work of this kind. For instance, the first part, which provides the workman with geometrical lines, applied to various purposes in the cabinet branch, cannot be subject to alteration any more than the principles of reason itself. The same may be said of Perspective; the subject of the second part. This art, being founded on Geometry and Optics, may be improved in its practice but its fundamental principles can never be altered, any more than the nature of vision itself.

As to the designs in furniture contained in part third, these are indeed liable to change; nor is it in the power of any man to provide against it, by making such drawings as will always be thought new. Yet the instructions given on the manufacturing part being founded on real experience and practice, will be much the same at all times. It also adds to the usefulness of the designs, that I have in general given their geometrical dimensions, either laid down on the ground, or other scale lines adapted for that purpose, or else described in the letterpress. So that no person, however ignorant of perspective, can easily mistake the perspective for the geometrical measurements, or be at any loss to know the general sizes of such pieces as shall be introduced.

In proceeding however, with the first edition, I found that to give scales for the perspective heights and widths could not be done, in many instances, without encumbering the designs in such a way as greatly to hurt their appearance. To remove this inconvenience, and to assist those who have a little knowledge of perspective, in obtaining the true measurements of such designs or engravings as may have no scales to them, I have shewn, in the perspective part, that this may be easily done, by finding the vanishing points and distance, and tracing their visuals forward to the ground line. In the first edition this is done at the end of the Appendix, because its usefulness did not strike me till I came to that part of the work.

With respect to mouldings and various ornaments, the subject of the fourth part, it is granted that these are of a changeable kind. Yet it is pretty evident that materials for proper ornaments are now brought to such perfection as will not, in future, admit of much, if any, degree of improvement, though they may, by the skill and touch of the ingenious hand, be varied, ad infinitum, to suit any taste at any time.

Lastly, I would entreat leave gratefully to acknowledge the general encouragement I have been favoured with in going through the first edition: and though my vast expense has deprived me of the emolument that might have been expected for so numerous a subscription, yet it is some consolation to be conscious that I have spared no expense, nor withheld anything in my power to do the work justice, and give satisfaction to the public.

PREFACE

And I have the additional happiness to know, from several testimonies, the full approbation that the work has obtained in the judgment of the candid and skilful. And, notwithstanding the ill nature of some, who hate to speak well of anything but their own productions, I only wish that a comparison be made with any other book hitherto published for the use of Cabinet-makers and Upholsterers, and then it will sufficiently speak for itself.

And now, in going through this third edition, it is still my steady intention to contribute as much as I can towards improving the work, and rendering it as complete as is in the power of,

Gentlemen,

Your humble Servant,

THOMAS SHERATON.

CONTENTS

SHERATON

THE CABINET-MAKER AND UPHOLSTERER'S DRAWING-BOOK

SHERATON

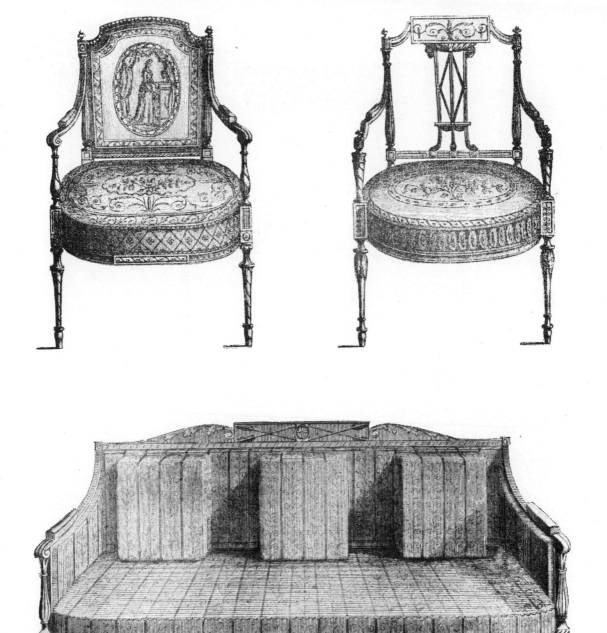

Drawing-Room Chairs and Sofa

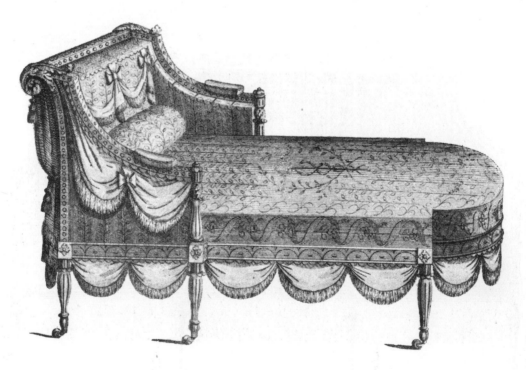

Chaises Longues

SHERATON

Conversation Chairs and Sofa

SHERATON

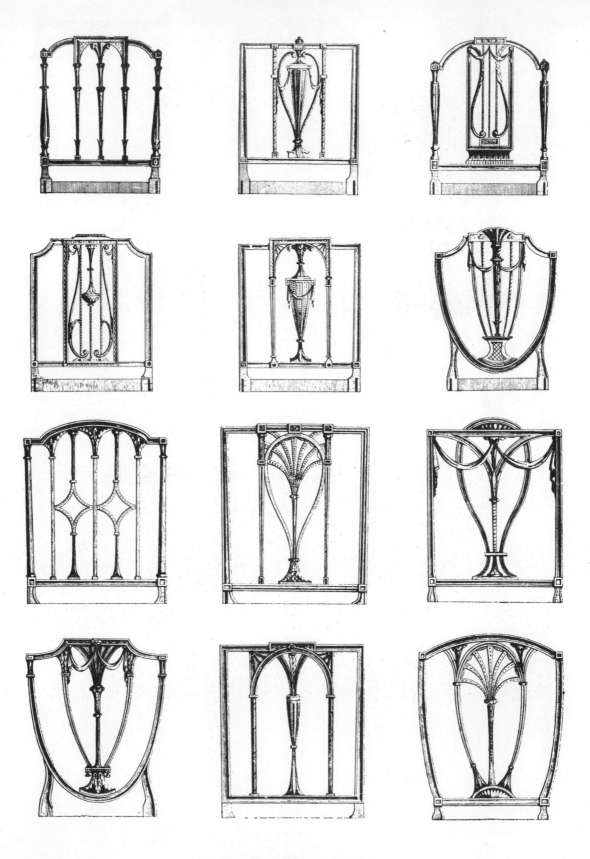

Backs for Parlour Chairs

SHERATON

Backs for Painted Chairs

SHERATON

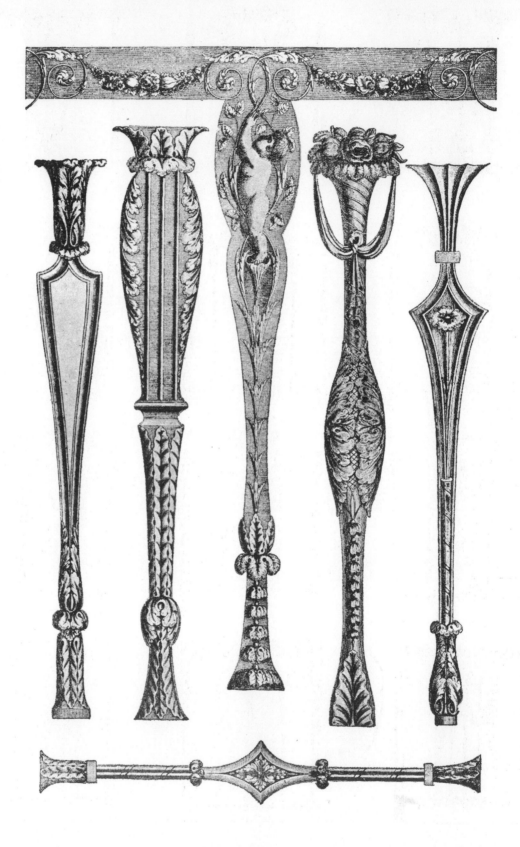

Splads for Painted and Mahogany Chairs

SHERATON

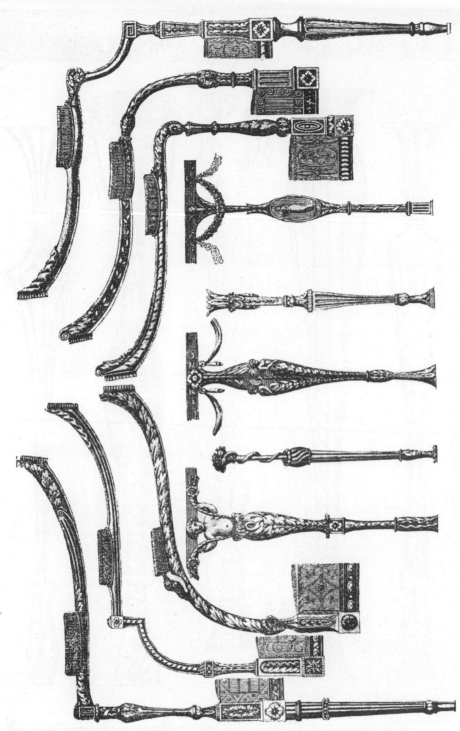

Stumps and Elbows for Drawing-Room Chairs

SHERATON

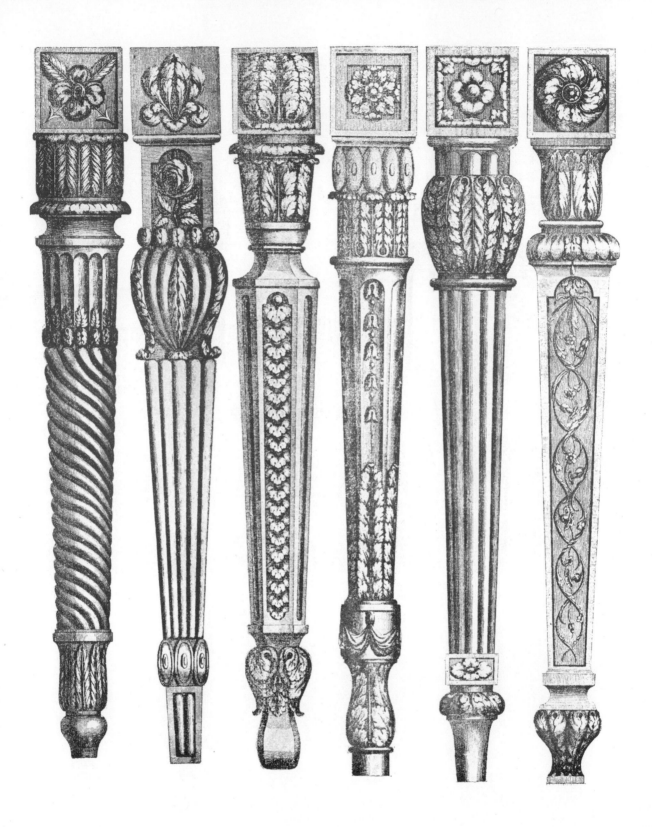

Chair Legs

SHERATON

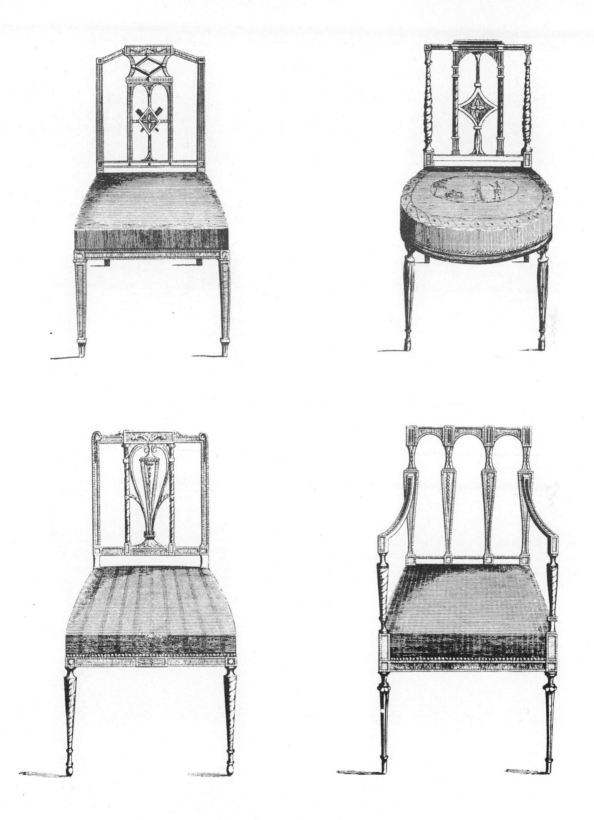

Three Parlour Chairs and a Drawing-room Chair

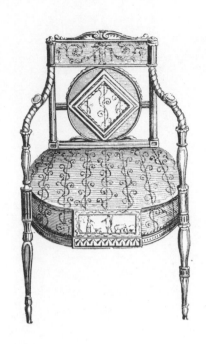

Drawing-room Chairs and Pier Tables

SHERATON

A Drawing Table, a Cabinet, and Tripod Candlestands

SHERATON

A Commode Dressing Table, a Chamber-horse, a Lady's Dressing Writing Table,
a Writing Table, and a Cylinder Desk and Bookcase

SHERATON

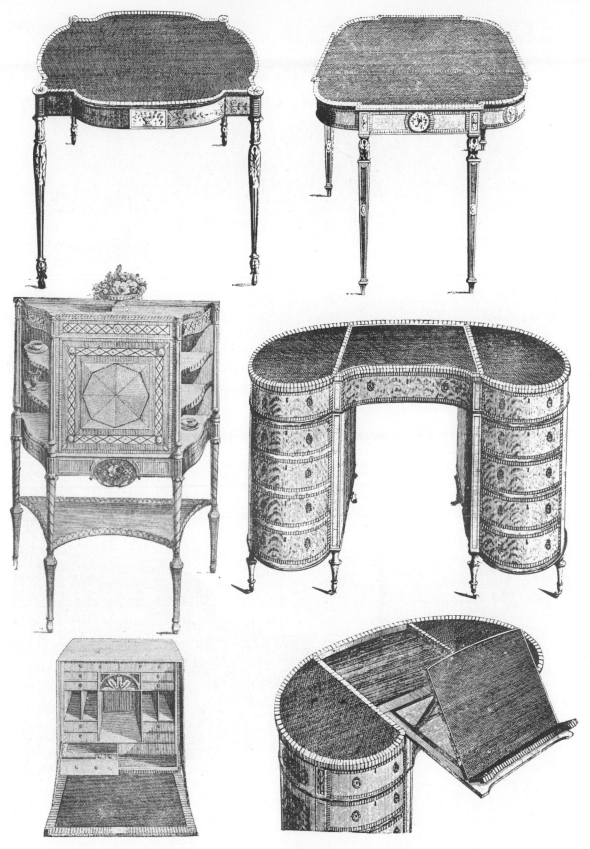

Card Tables, Lady's Cabinet, showing inside fittings, and a Kidney Table

Ornament for a Table, Secretary and Bookcase, and Clock Cases

SHERATON

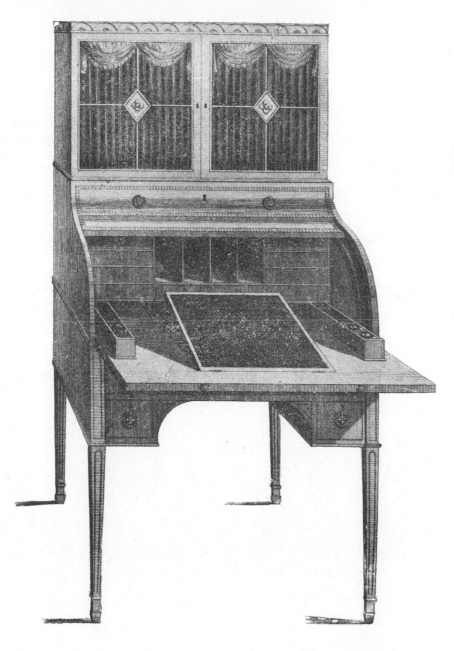

Border for a Pier Table, and a Cylinder Desk and Bookcase

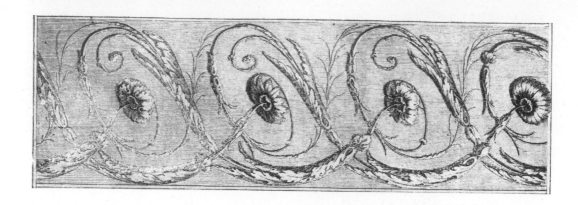

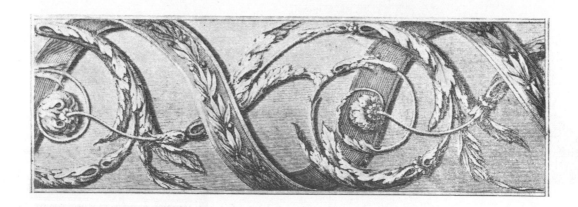

Borders for Pier Tables

SHERATON

Bookcase and Writing Drawers, Drawing Table, Lady's Secretary with carved front, and Library Steps and Pembroke Table

SHERATON

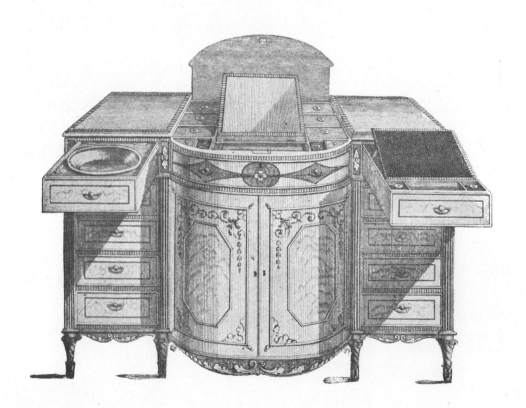

A Library Table and a Lady's Dressing Commode

SHERATON

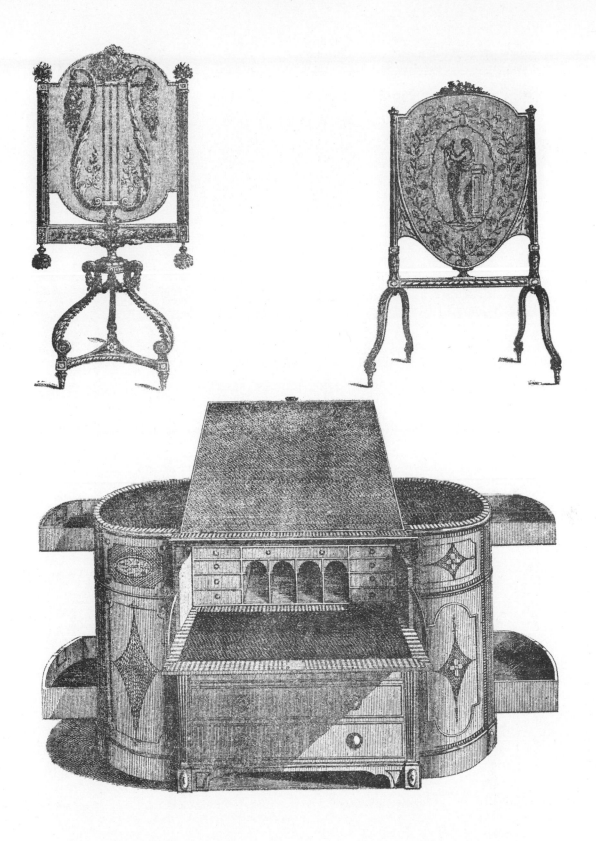

Horse Fire Screens and a Library Table with Secretary Drawers

SHERATON

Various Leaves and Bookcase Doors

SHERATON

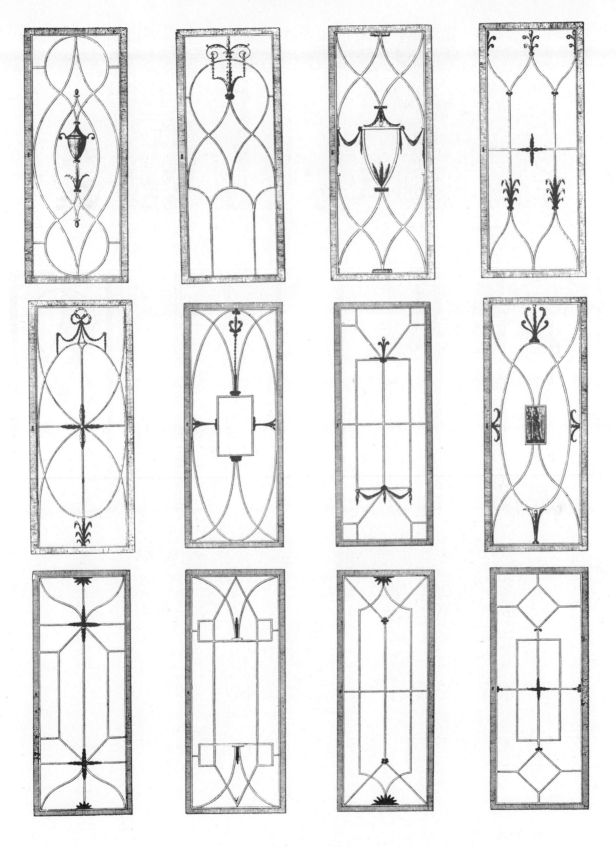

Bookcase Doors

SHERATON

New Bed-steps, a Bidet Dressing Table, and a Night-Table Basin-stand

SHERATON

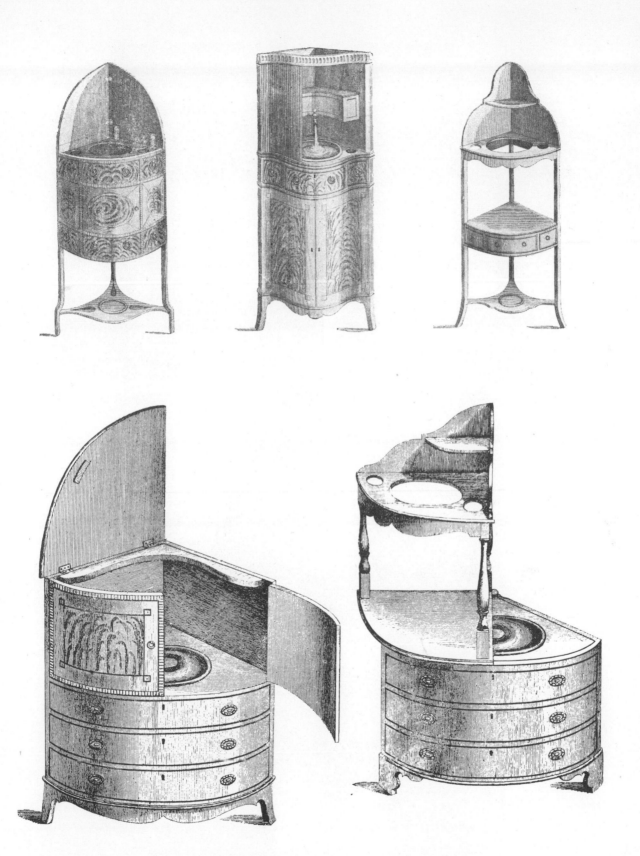

Corner Basin-stands and Corner Night Tables

SHERATON

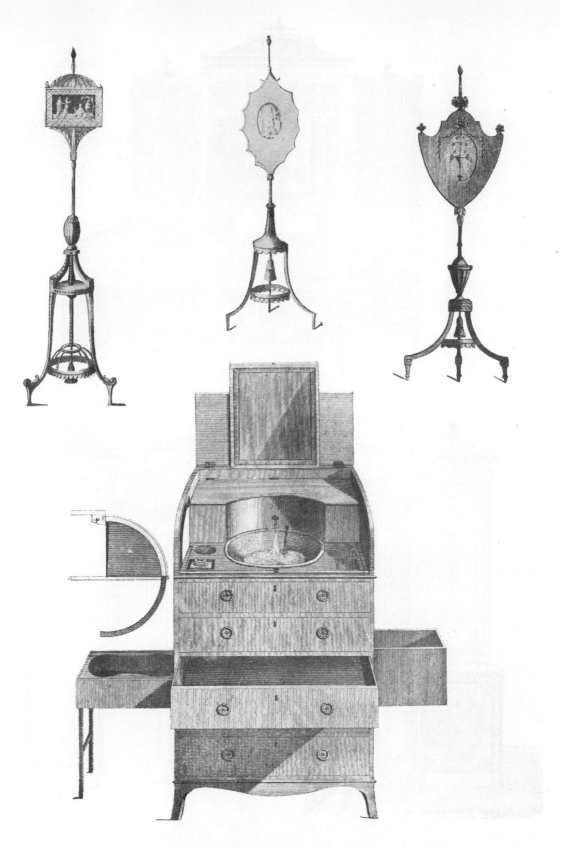

Tripod Fire Screens and a Cylinder Wash-hand Table

SHERATON

A Gentleman's Secretary and a Library Case

SHERATON

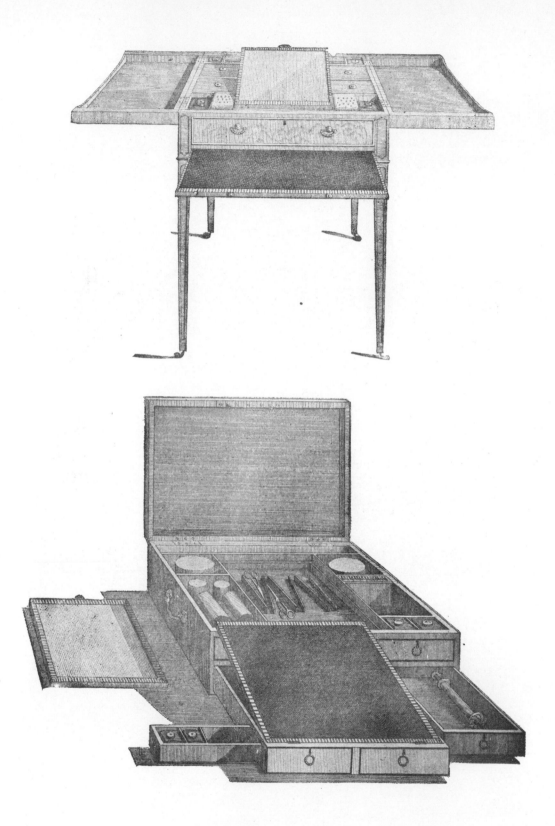

Dressing Table and a Lady's Travelling Box

SHERATON

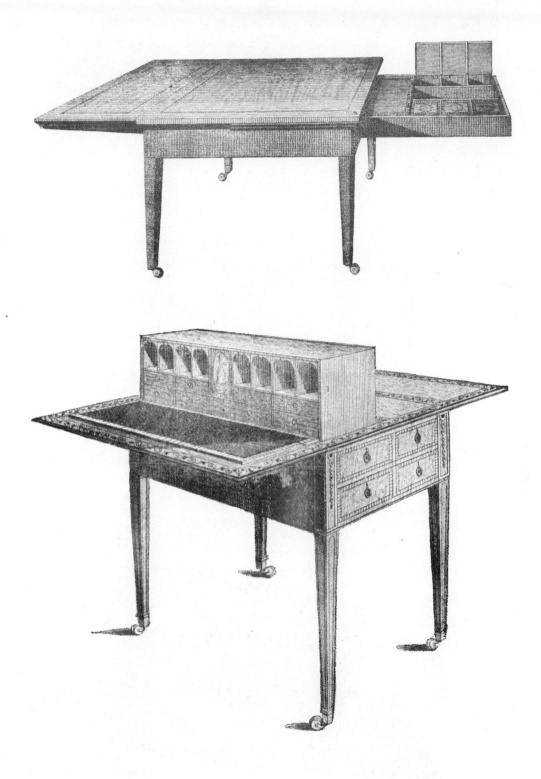

The Universal Table and a Harlequin Pembroke Table

SHERATON

A Cabinet and a Dressing Chest

SHERATON

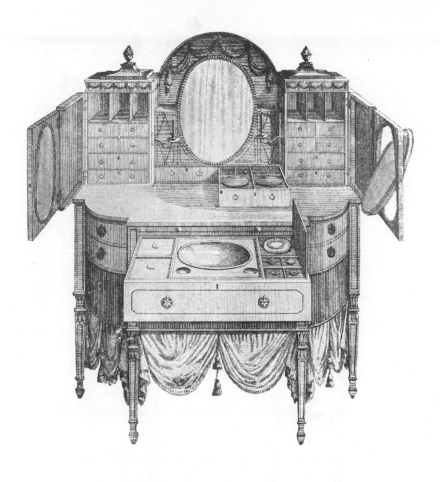

A Lady's Combined Dressing Table and a Dressing Chest

SHERATON

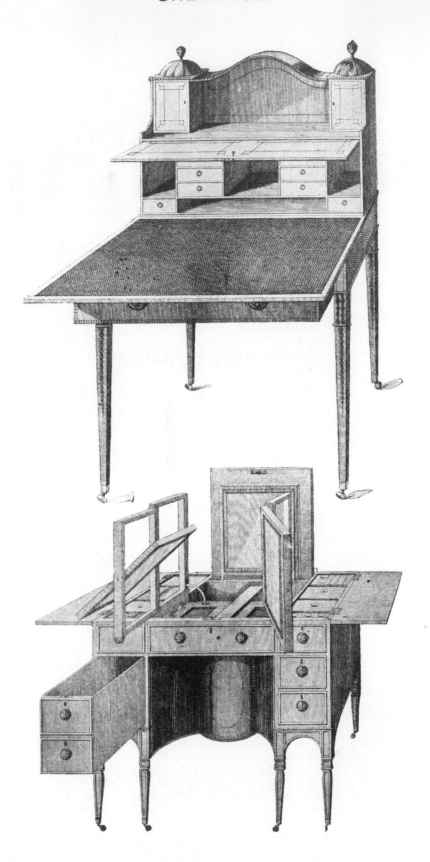

Lady's Cabinet and Writing Table, and Lady's Dressing Table

SHERATON

A Screen Table, a Wash Stand, a Lady's Secretary, a Pot Cupboard

SHERATON

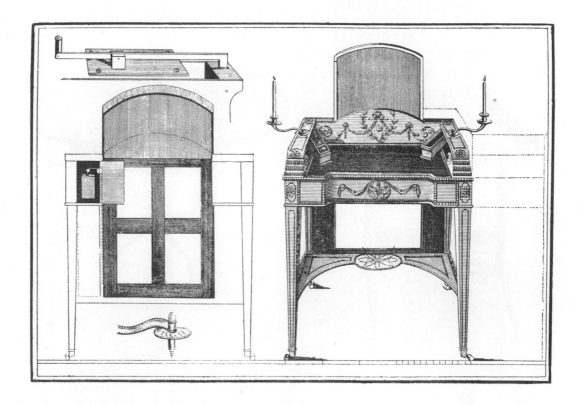

Horse Dressing Glass and Writing Table, Horse Dressing Glass,
and a Lady's Writing Table

SHERATON

Ladies' Work-Tables and a Pembroke Table

SHERATON

Sideboard, showing Spring for Secret Drawer, and a Sideboard Table

SHERATON

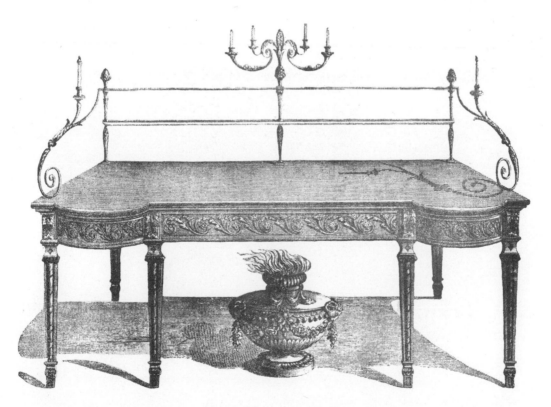

Sideboard with Vase Knife-cases, and Sideboard with Mahogany Vase
underneath to hold Bottles

SHERATON

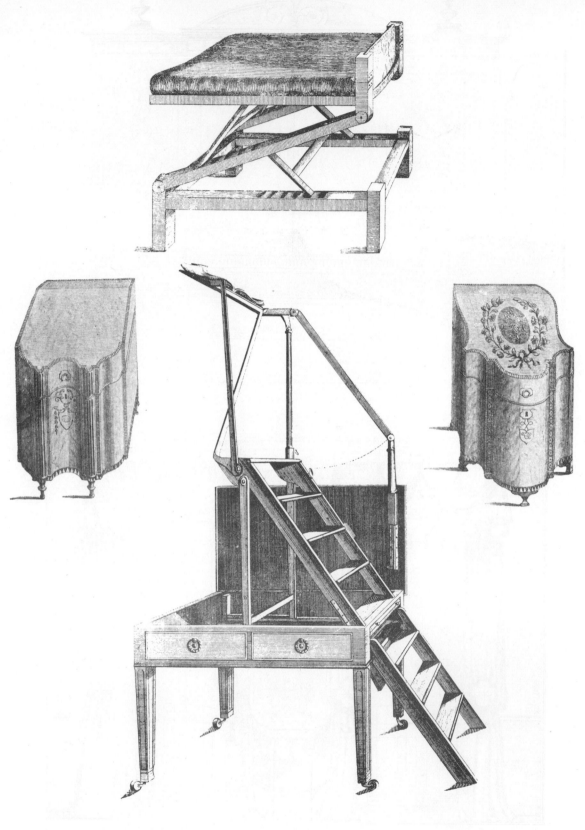

A Gouty Stool, Knife-cases, and Library Steps and Table

SHERATON

A Wardrobe, and Cornices, Curtains, and Drapery for Drawing-Room Windows

The Two Ends of a Drawing-Room

SHERATON

The Two Sides of a Drawing-Room

A View of the Prince of Wales's Chinese Drawing-Room
View of south end of same Room

SHERATON

A Commode

SHERATON

An English State Bed

A Sofa Bed

A French State Bed, obliquely situated to the picture; and an Elliptic Bed for a single Lady

SHERATON

A Duchesse

A Design for a Bed

SHERATON

A Summer Bed in two Compartments

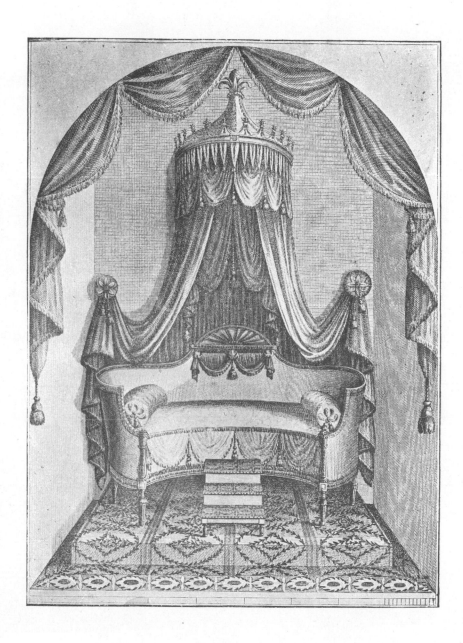

An Alcove Bed

SHERATON

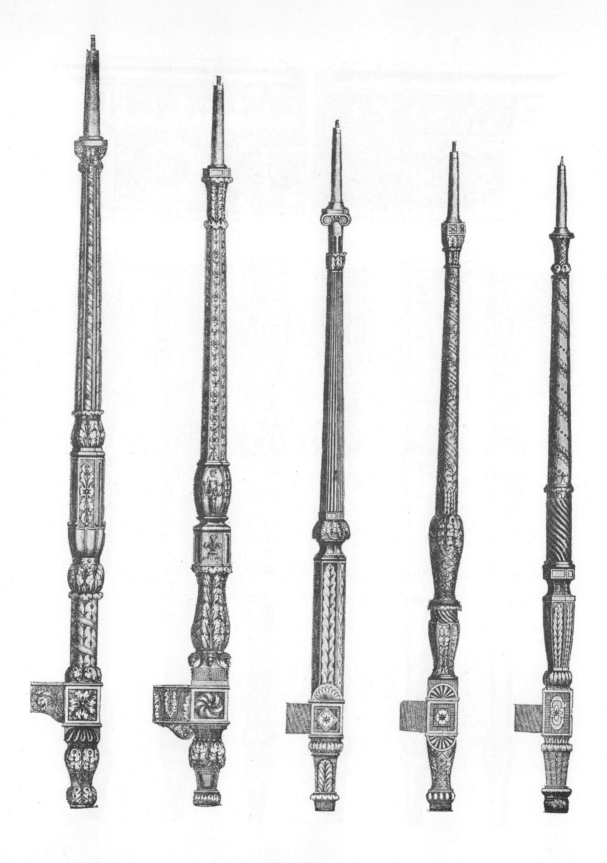

Bed Pillars

SHERATON

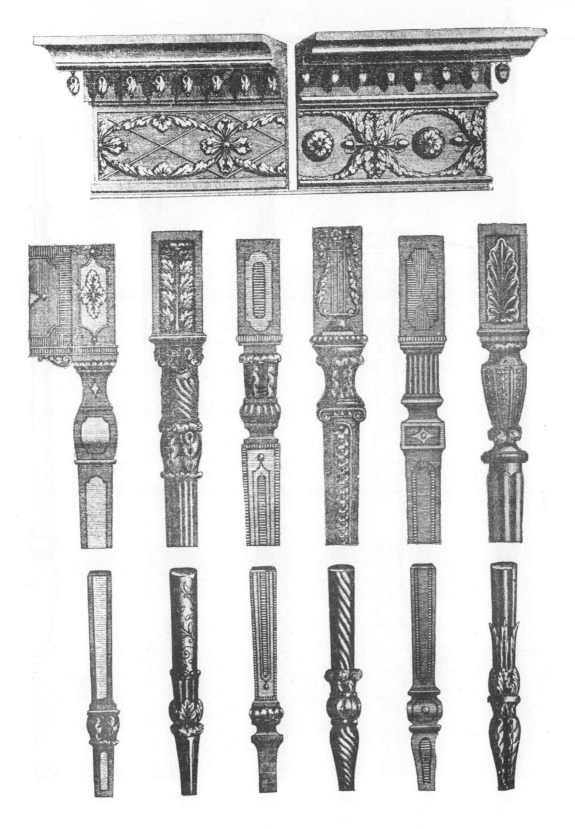

Cornices for Friezes, and Legs for Pier and Card Tables

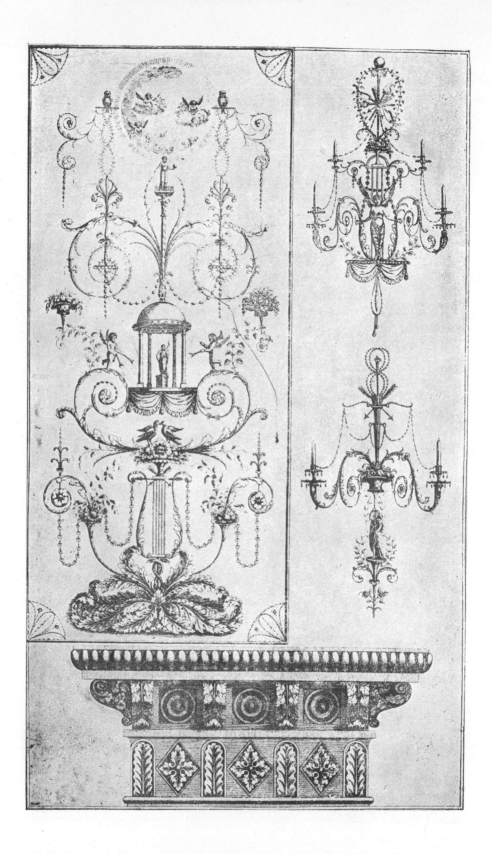

Ornament for a Painted Panel, Girandoles, and a Cornice
and Frieze for a Pilaster

Ornament for a Frieze or Tablet

SHERATON

Pilasters for Commodes

SHERATON

Window Cornices

SHERATON

Specimens of Ornament for the exercise of Learners

SHERATON

Pediments for Bookcases, and Centres for Pembroke Tables

SHERATON

A Dining Parlour, in imitation of the Prince of Wales's, a Pulpit,
Tuscan Pedestal, Tuscan Entablature and Capital

SHERATON

THE FIVE ORDERS

Tuscan Doric Ionic Composite or Corinthian
Roman

DESIGNS FOR
HOUSEHOLD FURNITURE

DESIGNS

FOR

HOUSEHOLD FURNITURE

EXHIBITING A VARIETY OF

ELEGANT AND USEFUL PATTERNS

IN THE

Cabinet, Chair, and Upholstery Branches

ON EIGHTY-FOUR PLATES

⸻

BY THE LATE

T. SHERATON

CABINET-MAKER

⸻

LONDON

PUBLISHED BY J. TAYLOR

AT THE ARCHITECTURAL LIBRARY

Nº· 59 HIGH HOLBORN

1812

CONTENTS

DESIGNS FOR HOUSEHOLD FURNITURE

SHERATON

Parlour Chairs

SHERATON

Parlour and Drawing-Room Chairs

SHERATON

Parlour and Drawing-Room Chairs

SHERATON

Herculaneums, Drawing-Room and Parlour Chairs

SHERATON

A Tub or Easy-Chair
A Cabriolet Arm-Chair
A Parlour Chair

Library Steps
Chair Bed

A Fauteuil Chair
A Hunting Chair
A Parlour Chair

SHERATON

Camp Chair   Camp Table   Bergère Chair

Masonic Chair   Reading Chair

Nelson's Chairs

SHERATON

Corridor Chair, Conversation Chair, Curricules, and Grecian Sofa

SHERATON

Sofas

SHERATON

Grecian Couches

SHERATON

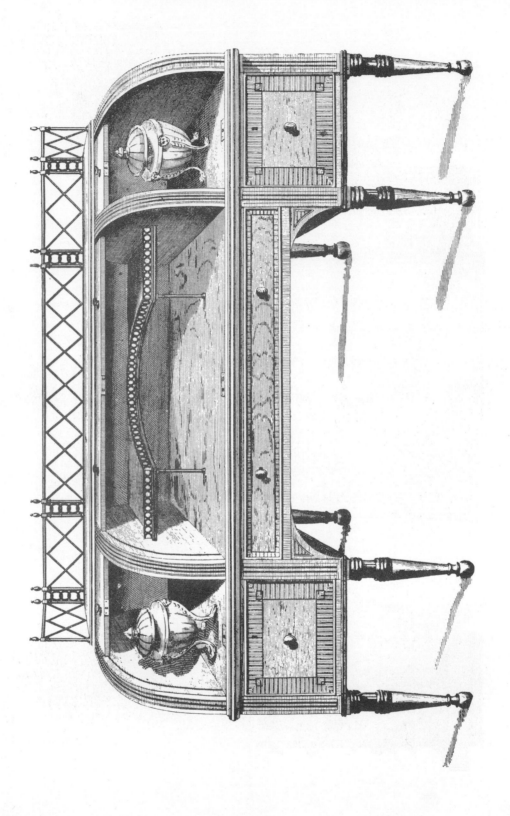

Sideboard

SHERATON

Side-Table and Sideboard

SHERATON

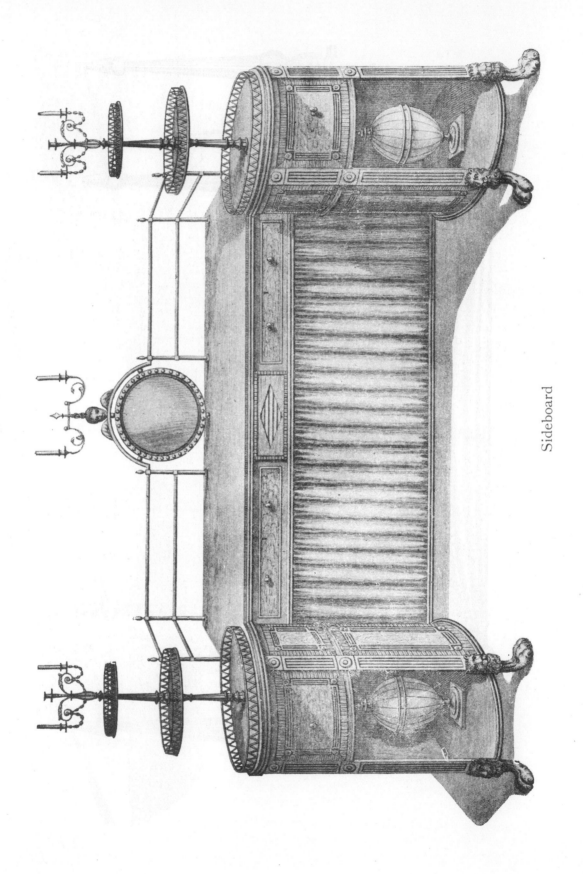

Sideboard

SHERATON

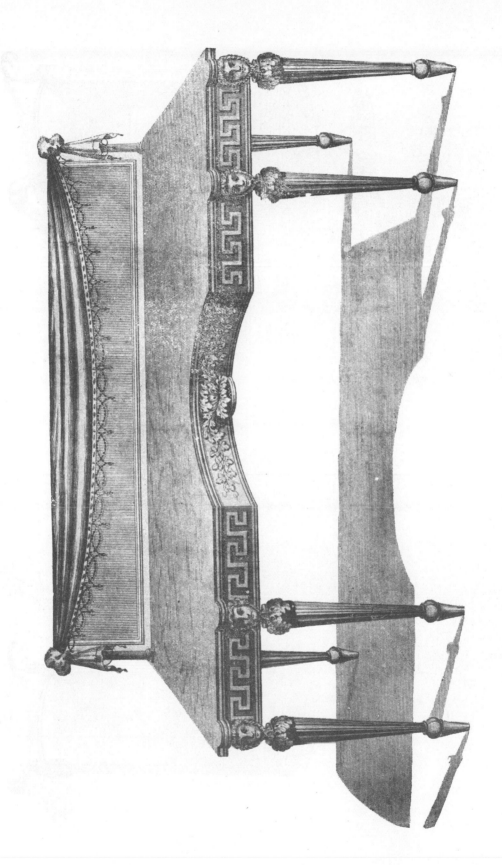

Side-Table

SHERATON

Side-Table and Sideboard

SHERATON

Pier Tables

SHERATON

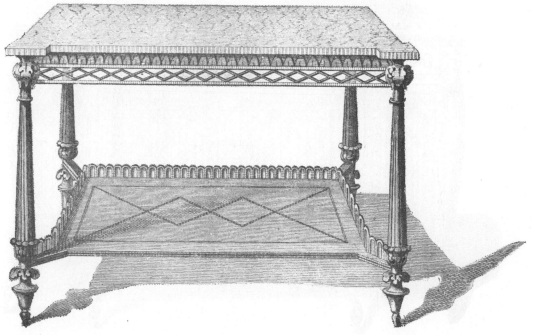

A Commode and a Pier Table

SHERATON

A Cabinet and a Commode

SHERATON

Cabinet and Quartetto Table

SHERATON

Lady's Writing and Dressing Table

SHERATON

Lady's Writing and Dressing Table, and Dumb Waiters

SHERATON

Dressing Commode and Pier Table

SHERATON

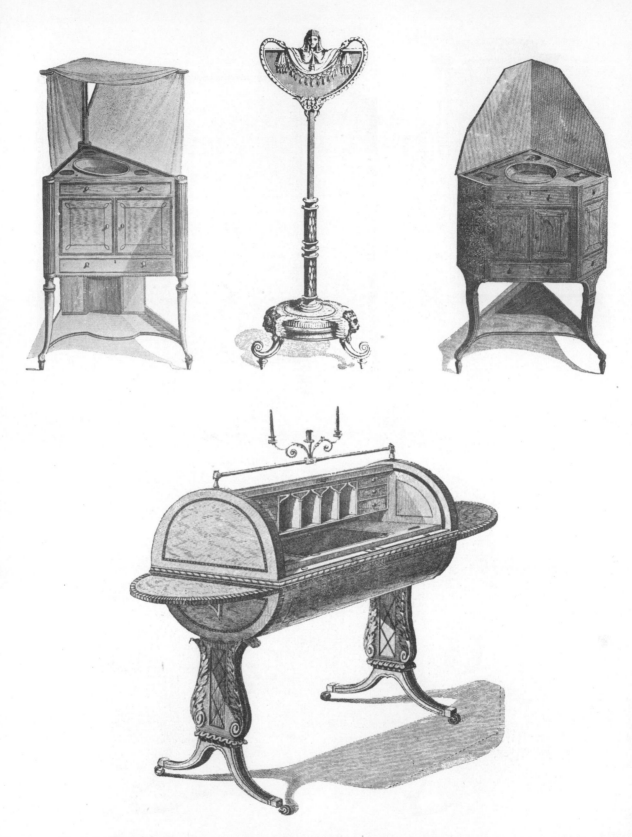

Corner Wash-hand Stand, Tripod Fire Screen, and Cylinder Writing Table

SHERATON

Buffet, Fire Screen, and Sofa Table

SHERATON

Sofa Table and Library Table

SHERATON

Loo Table and Sofa Table

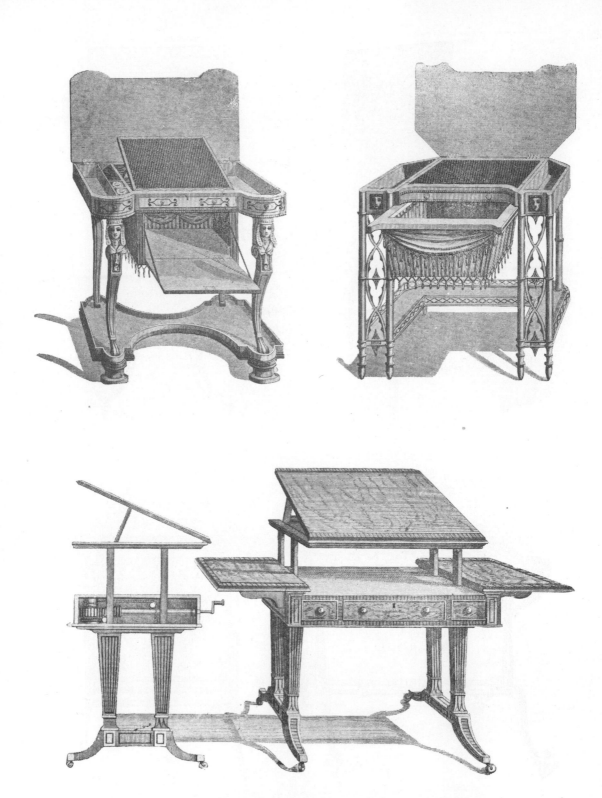

Ladies' Work Tables and Sofa Writing Table

SHERATON

Ladies' Work Tables and Pouch Tables

SHERATON

Dumb Waiters, Gentleman's Secretary, and Lady's Writing Table

SHERATON

Horseshoe
Writing Table

Gentleman's Shaving Table and Occasional Table

SHERATON

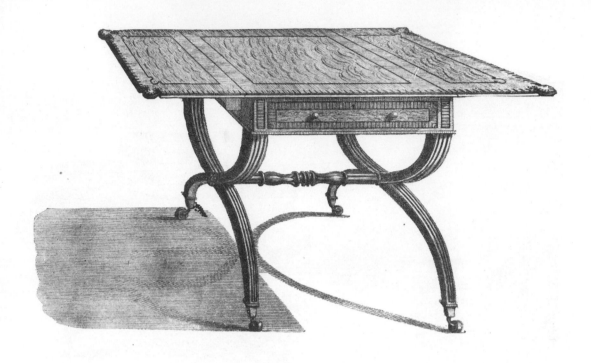

Pembroke Table, Dressing Table

Bureau Bookcase, Library Tables, and Moving Bookcase

Library Table

SHERATON

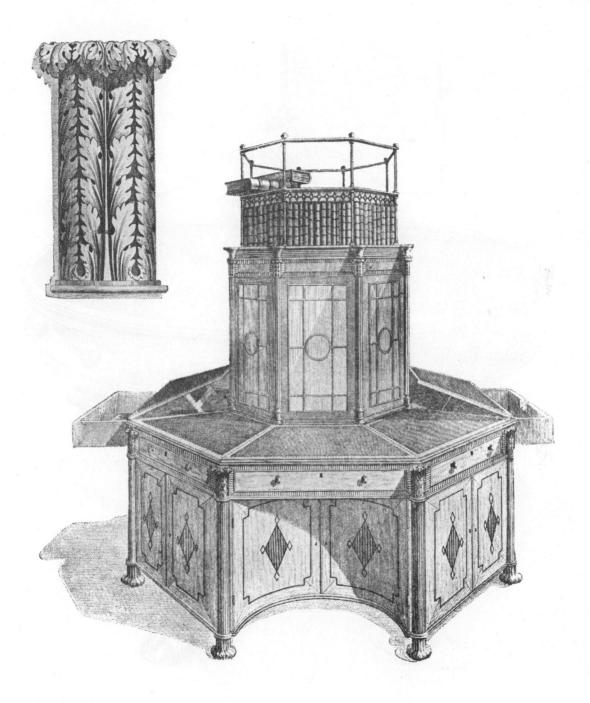

Octagon Library Table

SHERATON

New Design for a Dining Table

SHERATON

Secretary and Bookcase

SHERATON

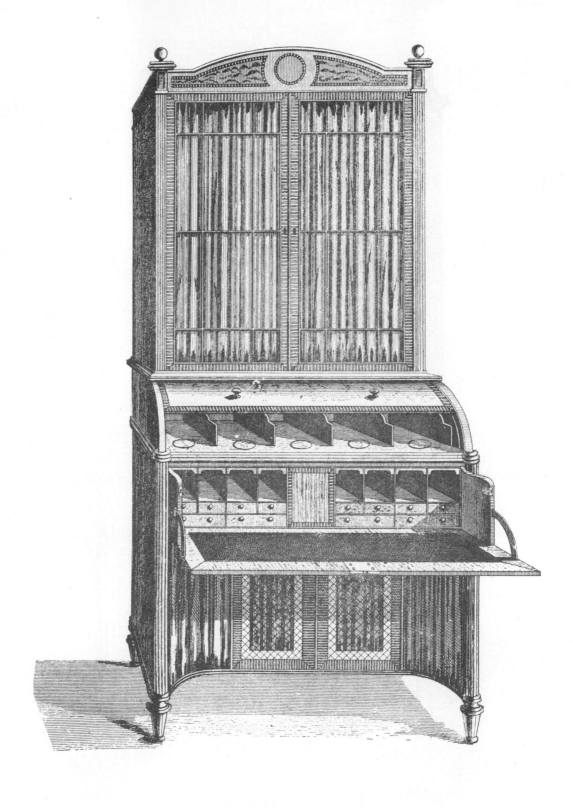

Secretary and Bookcase

SHERATON

Secretary and Bookcase

SHERATON

Bookcase

SHERATON

Bookcase

SHERATON

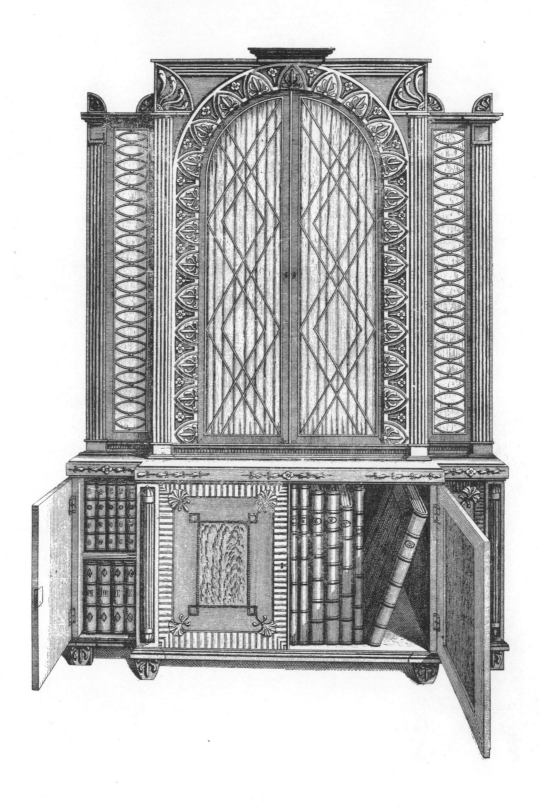

Bookcase

SHERATON

Cylinder Bookcase

SHERATON

Bookcase and Library-case

SHERATON

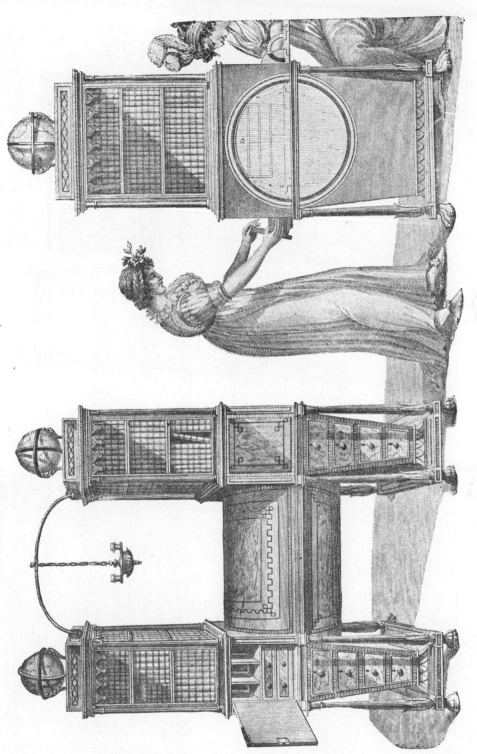

Sisters' Cylinder Bookcase

SHERATON

Bookcase Doors

SHERATON

Gothic Light   Chinese Light

SHERATON

A New Design for a Bed

SHERATON

A New Design for a Bed

SHERATON

Design for a Bed

SHERATON

Design for a Bed

SHERATON

French Bed

SHERATON

French Bed

A Grecian Bed

SHERATON

Alcove Bed

SHERATON

Canopy Bed

SHERATON

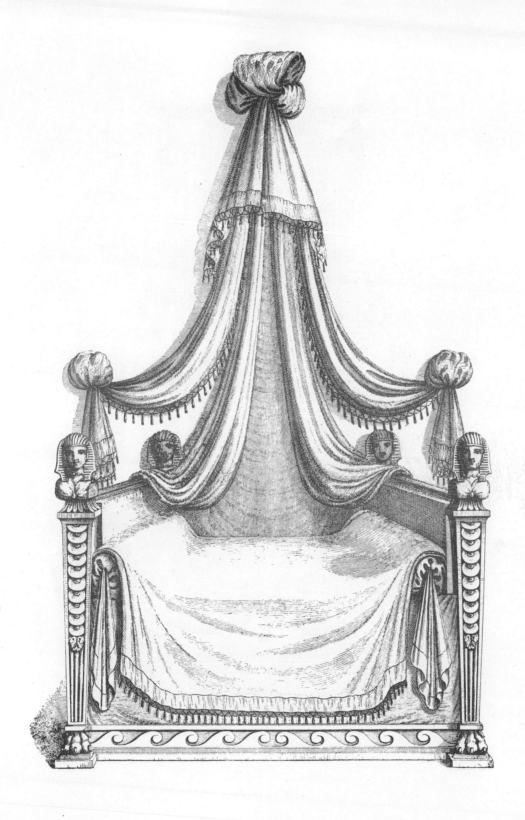

Canopy Bed

SHERATON

State Bed

SHERATON

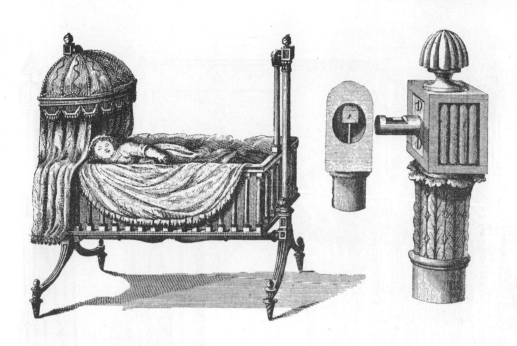

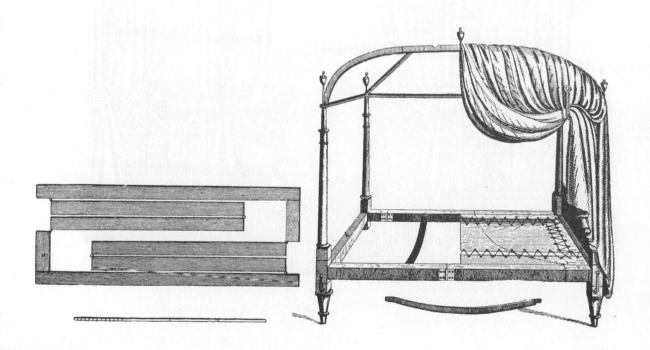

A Swinging Crib Bed   Camp Bed

SHERATON

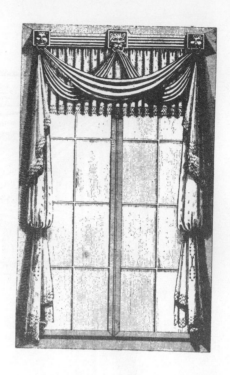

Window and Pier Glass Draperies, and Sofa-Bed

SHERATON

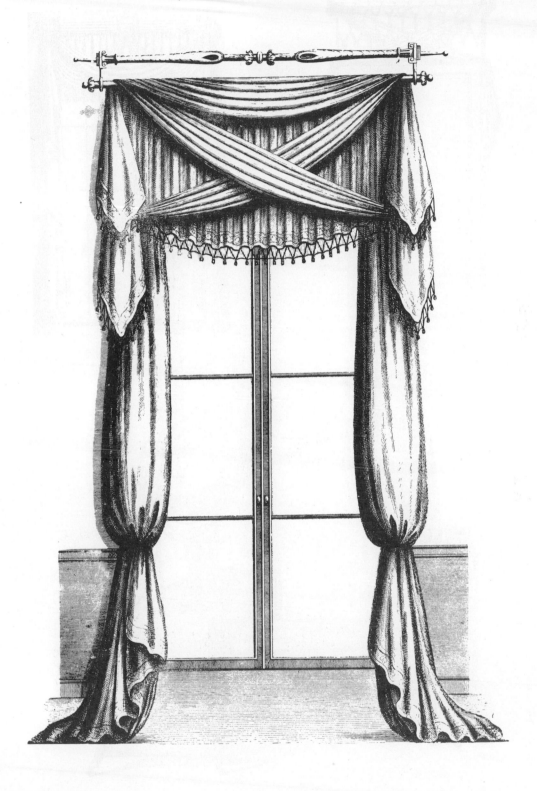

Window Draperies

SHERATON

Window Draperies

SHERATON

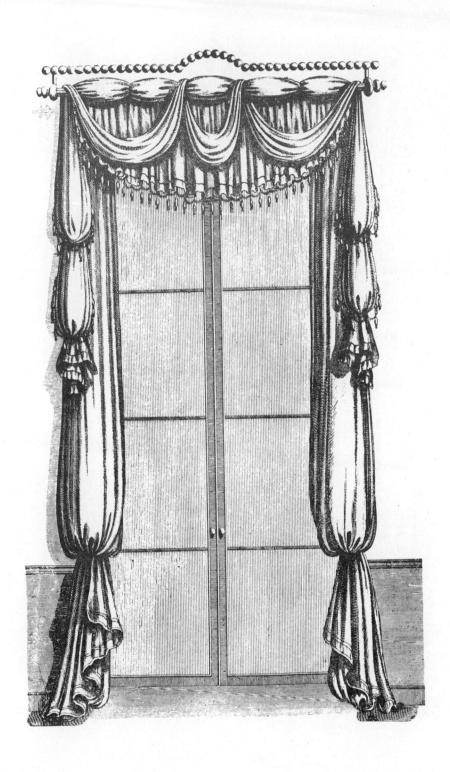

New Window Draperies

SHERATON

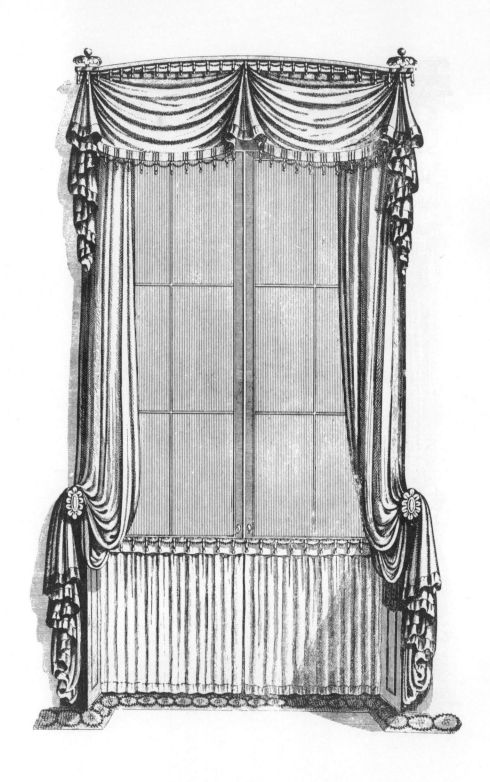

New French Window Draperies

SHERATON

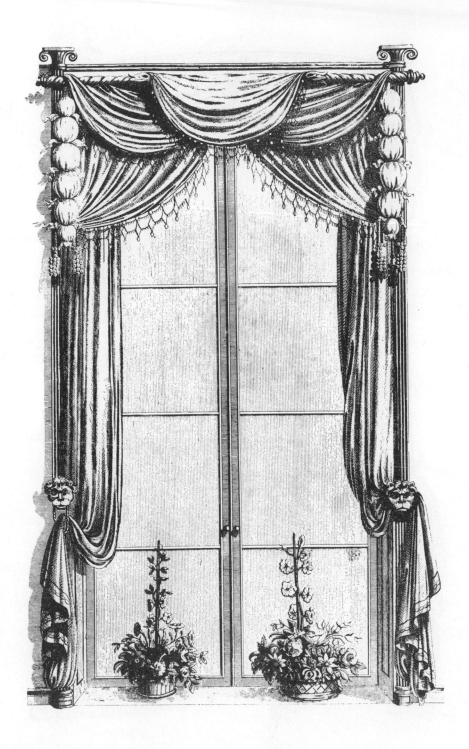

Window Draperies

SHERATON

Window Drapery and Drawing-Room Chair

SHERATON

Window Drapery

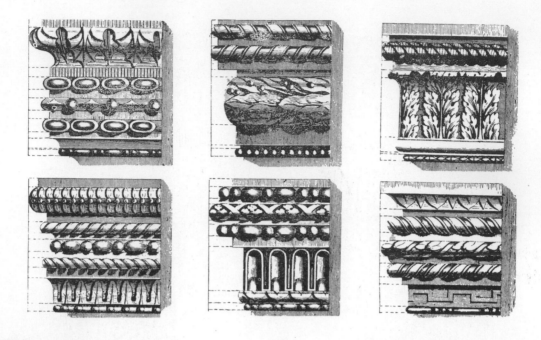

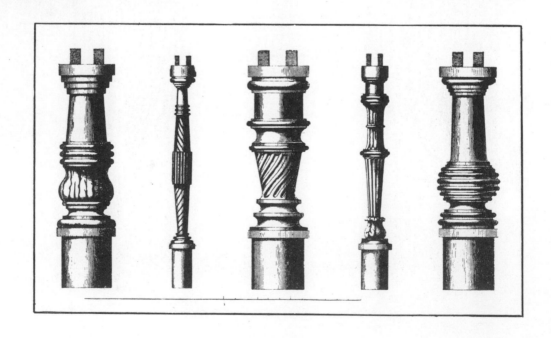

Mouldings for Architraves and Window Cornices, and Pillars for Tables